To my husband, Matt,
and our four children:
Caryn, Ammon, Joseph, and Benjamin,
who make every day a fun adventure.

- Tristi

For my wife and best friend, Tiffani,
and my sweet baby girl, Elianna.
Thanks for all the hugs, kisses, and silliness
that make me laugh every day.

- Brett

To Erika, To Zachary, To Zoe, To Xander,
who have supported me in this
amazing journey called life,
and who help me confront each day
as if it were my last.

- Ethan

MILLION DOLLAR DIVA

The Smart Woman's Guide to Getting Rich Safely

TRISTI PINKSTON
BRETT KITCHEN
ETHAN KAP

Golden Wings Enterprises

This publication is designed to provide accurate and authoritative information in regard to the subject matter covered. It is sold with the understanding that authors and publisher are not engaged in rendering legal or accounting services. If legal or other expert assistance is required, the services of a competent professional should be sought.

MILLION DOLLAR DIVA:
The Smart Woman's Guide to Getting Rich Safely

Published by:
Golden Wings Enterprises
PO Box 468
Orem, UT 84059

ISBN: 978-0-9794340-5-1

Printed in the United States of America
Year of First Printing: 2012

CONTENTS

Special Note to Reader

This book is *not* intended to give any tax or investment advice of any kind. Neither is it intended to make or suggest any personal recommendation as to what any individual should or shouldn't choose in regard to the most fitting and appropriate financial strategy. Each woman's needs and situations are as unique as her own fingerprint. Also—and we point this out multiple times throughout this book—while these strategies exist as of the writing of this manuscript, no one can guarantee that they will exist in the future.

Therefore, we encourage you to seek professional advice from a knowledgeable representative who fully understands these concepts and can not only provide you the most up-to-date information, but clearly outline both the benefits, as well as the pitfalls, of this or any other strategy you might pursue.

Lastly, we urge each reader to pursue only what is in her specific and best interest. The intent of this book is solely to introduce some of the unique and powerful concepts and strategies that are available, if utilized to their full potential.

We hope you enjoy the journey.

- Brett Kitchen & Ethan Kap

Chapter 1

DANGEROUS JUNGLES AND BEAUTIFUL FLOWERS

"Semitruck! Semitruck! Semitruck!" My friend Jenni panicked as her car slipped on the road.

My eyes were squeezed tight, but I could sense Jenni scrambling to get control of the steering wheel. Just seconds before, we had hit a patch of black ice, and although Jenni fought it, we had been thrown into a U-turn right into oncoming traffic—right into the path of a semi.

"We've got to get out of the way," she said. I felt the car move to the side and Jenni's exhale of relief, and then I felt something else—impact with the back bumper. I was thrown forward, and then back. We spun around again, and my side of the car smacked into the semi. My head struck the door, hard, then bounced over again to the left as the car continued to spin. Nothing was real—and it all seemed to be happening so slowly.

I'd said nothing during this time. As soon as we went into the U-turn, I'd closed my eyes—it's better not to see things sometimes—and offered up one thought: "Heavenly Father . . ." Everything began to fade to black. As I pulled back to consciousness, my next full thought was, "I want my chiropractor."

I opened my eyes and could see the shattered windshield in front of me, yet everything was blurry. My glasses had flown off my face. Jenni was checking my pulse, my pupils—it's handy when the driver of the car is a trained first responder.

"Don't die, Tristi. Please, please don't die," she kept saying.

I wanted to tell her I was just fine, but forming words was hard, and my head hurt. I mean, it really, really hurt. "I haven't died yet," I said at last, referencing the fact that I've been in several car accidents over the course of my lifetime. "I'm not going to do it now."

"The engine's smoking. We've got to get you out of here," she told me. I looked at my door, so crumpled that I could tell from the inside how badly damaged it was. I reached out and pulled on the handle, a feeble attempt. It wouldn't budge.

I thought about crawling over the driver's seat and out. I tried to move, but my muscles wouldn't let me.

Just then, the paramedics arrived. A couple of men lifted the hood of the car and started frantically cutting wires and taking apart the engine. Another man came around to my side and started talking to me. He pried my door open just enough to slip his arm through and cup my neck with his hand. Then other men pulled my door the rest of the way off, bending it backwards on its hinges. I was then treated to my first backboard, my first neck collar, and my first ambulance ride. I was a little disappointed that they didn't use the Jaws of Life. That would have been pretty cool.

Jenni found my glasses folded neatly, perfectly safe, in the center of the back seat, of all the strange places to find them. The side of my face, while it felt like a giant black eye, was only a little swollen, and not bruised at all. I had no seatbelt abrasions, although I felt like I should have had a three-foot-long rope burn. My neck was not cracked or broken, as proven by a CAT scan—my very first, another thing to add to my list of new adventures. I can't tell this story without pausing to say that I know for a fact we were protected through divine intervention. There's no logical way we survived, and yet, we came out of it without a single mark on us.

* * *

We all have challenges, and sometimes we feel as though we've been hit by a semitruck. It's not everyone who can say that and mean it literally. Jenni and I have joked that we should write a corny self-help book—"In twelve easy steps, we'll show you how you can walk away from the semitruck in your life, how you can cast off the backboard of disbelief, the neck collar of negativity, and come out a winner!" Joking aside, life does throw challenges at us. Sometimes we're blessed to walk away from them, and sometimes we have to work through them, one painful day after another, until we find our solutions. These issues can be financial, emotional, spiritual—we are tested in all areas of our lives, and it can be immensely helpful to find someone who knows the ropes to guide us through it.

Strangely enough, I had just started writing this very book with best-selling authors Brett Kitchen and Ethan Kap before my accident. They were pretty relieved to hear that their co-author hadn't just been killed, and they immediately began thinking of ways to help me deal with the aftermath—you'll see a lot of that as we continue through the book. My wellbeing was their top priority in the project, and I appreciate that.

After I got home from the emergency room, I was overwhelmed with gratitude for how things had turned out—but I was also overwhelmed with something else. Pain. True, I had no broken bones or visible bruising, but my body had been tossed around like a sock in a washing machine, and I was really feeling it. As I climbed into my bed, my neck seized, and I had to hold on to my hair in order to lower my head to the pillow. I laughed, but I also realized that things weren't going to be the same for a long, long time.

We began a long circus of insurance claims and paperwork, and we also began our rehabilitation. Jenni and I had chosen to see the same doctor—the one I'd been wishing for as soon as I regained consciousness—and he told us we were both more injured than we knew. As we did our initial accident exam, this was confirmed—I had lost a lot of motor skill and strength on my left side, my spine was a total mess, my brain was struggling to function, and I was looking at a long road of recovery and therapy, as was Jenni.

We may think we've walked away from the semitrucks in our lives, but the ramifications can be long-lasting. I promise, this isn't going to be the corny self-help book I mentioned earlier, but the metaphor does fit—we're so happy that we came out of it relatively unscathed, but we had to stop and look at the real-life impact (oh, no . . . these puns are just going to keep popping up, aren't they . . .) it had on our lives. I had to stop everything I was doing for a while. I had to delay my clients. I had to turn the kids, the housework, and all my errands over to my husband. We had already been going through a heavy challenge— now there was this on top of it.

We weren't prepared for it, not at all.

* * *

As you take a look at your financial status, are you prepared for something completely unexpected to happen? If you were in an accident tomorrow and couldn't work for a week, two weeks, a month, what would that do to your overall picture? I'm writing this chapter six weeks after my accident, so yes, I am able to work, but I'm still at half capacity, and I have no way of knowing when I'll be back entirely. This accident has changed my life, my family's life, and it has changed how we do everything and think about everything. How will your challenges affect you? I sincerely hope you won't learn for yourself the joys of getting in a car accident with a semi, but I know you will have hard things to overcome—everyone does. And I would love to see you be prepared for those challenges by having a pocket of safety—a little bit of money in savings, the ability to shop and take fantastic vacations as you desire, and the knowledge that you are out of debt so you're not bowled over when your challenges come up. This is not to say that all challenges are financial, because some are not. However, a great many of them are, and those are the issues we'll be discussing in this book.

Money has to be one of the most complicated things we face in our lives, but with Brett and Ethan's help, I'm getting a better handle on it—and you can, too.

Follow me on my journey and watch as I face my debts and learn how to create a million-dollar retirement. I hope you'll learn a lot and be able to make the same important changes in your own life. You just need willingness to follow the steps you'll learn here. Brett and Ethan have been working in the finance industry for a long time, and they can share their knowledge with us. They'll be our guides through the dangerous jungle—but you know what I hear? The most dangerous jungles have the most beautiful flowers. The rewards will be worth it.

Chapter 2

DIGGING OUT OF THE MESS I'M IN

I'm not stupid. In fact, there are times when—I flatter myself—I'm pretty smart. But as anyone who has ever had money problems can tell you, you don't have to be stupid to get into debt.

I grew up just this side of poor, so I'm used to making do or doing without. When I got married, my husband, Matt, had just been fired from his job, and I had quit mine in order to relocate with him. So there we were, two unemployed people getting married and starting a life together. I scaled back my aspirations, and we pulled off our wedding for less than $800. It didn't look like the best beginning financially, but we were very much in love. Still are.

We're hard workers. We took the first two jobs we found—both of us in fast food—and started putting things back together. Within a couple of months, he'd found a better job, and I continued on where I was. I was the assistant manager, and I loved my co-workers, so it was a good fit for me.

Shortly thereafter, I got pregnant with our first child, and eventually quit my job. Trying to make it on my husband's better—but still not good—income was hard, but we were determined to make it. We had both been raised with the principle, "Spend less than you make, and save some for a rainy day." We were in total agreement on that point, but there was one problem. We weren't making enough for our basic necessities, let alone having anything to set aside. And it's not like we were living high on the hog, going out all the time, or buying things we didn't need—our lives were very simple. And yet there still wasn't enough, and now we had a beautiful baby girl to care for.

Matt was frustrated. He'd gone through college and taken out student loans to get his BA in science, thinking this would help him in the job market. Not one job he'd ever landed was in the field of science, and it seemed he had run up tens of thousands in debt to get an education that would never pay him back.

I was frustrated. I watched my husband work long hours, come home worn out, and we still struggled to buy things like diapers and food. We did cloth diapers for a while, and I have to say, I hated that with a passion I can't even begin to describe.

So what did we do? We did what a great many people have done. We started putting diapers and groceries on the credit card. We didn't want to do it—we wanted to remain as debt-free as possible—but I had made a commitment to stay home and raise my daughter instead of returning to work, and my husband's income just wasn't enough. Charging diapers grew into charging gas. Now in addition to the student loan repayment, we had a credit card bill, and we had a car payment, in addition to our rent. All this debt, and only $288.00 income per week.

Going into debt is easy. It happens when we let down our guard just a little, become distracted by other things, and forget to track our spending and our income. It's very much like gaining weight—something else I've experienced. When we're busy and just go from day to day focusing on our tasks, things can get out of control, and then we have a wake-up call of some kind. In order to make a change, we have to look at ourselves long and hard, identify where we need to improve, and then make consistent daily choices to do better. Getting into debt is easy; getting out of debt takes effort. But just like losing weight—again, something I've experienced losing 84 pounds in the past eight months—as you learn to watch yourself and track your spending, you can get the situation back under control.

Matt and I have never really gotten on top of the financial game. We're still paying on student loans and credit cards—used to purchase other necessities when we experienced periods of unemployment or unusually high numbers of hungry children. For the most part, however, we've remained afloat. We've felt a little pinched from time to time, but always managed to pull it through. I started a company working from home, and have been able to contribute to the family income in that way. We're not rich, but we weren't worried.

Well, okay, we're worried now.

Things change.

The middle of this last year brought a change into our lives that we didn't expect. One of our four children was diagnosed with some severe health problems, and as he was treated, we discovered that many of the things that are ailing him run in our family. Before we knew it, we were all being treated, and I learned I have health issues I never even dreamed I had. I've always struggled with my health, but I didn't know how sick I really was. As we've embarked on our course of treatment, we've put all our money into paying our doctor and purchasing the healthy foods we should be consuming. And we started to worry as we began to juggle this bill to pay that bill, and working frantically to meet each new expectation.

Right in the middle of all this . . . I got hit by a semi.

Does any of this sound familiar to you? You think you've got things pretty well under control, you're doggy-paddling along, and then something happens and throws you a curve ball? I don't think I'm too far off the mark when I say that many of us live our lives this way. We're fine as long as nothing happens to rock the boat, but the first wave can capsize us.

As luck would have it—but I actually don't believe in luck, I believe in mercy—I got an e-mail from Brett Kitchen the very week I started to panic, and, as I mentioned, shortly before my car accident.

I had worked with Brett previously on the book he wrote with his business partner, Ethan Kap— the book that would take them to bestseller status, *Safe Money Millionaire*. Brett had mentioned their desire to write a financial book for women and asked me if I'd be interested in co-authoring. I love projects like that and said yes, but my schedule was so crazy, I hadn't been able to set up a meeting time. This e-mail from Brett reminded me of our agreement and brought a ray of hope along with it. A financial book for women, filled with advice written in a down-to-earth, easy-to-follow way, and I could learn about getting out of debt as we wrote it. I could actually pick Brett and Ethan's brains as to how I could maximize my income, and do it not just for a book, but so I could put it to use in my everyday life.

As you read this book, you will learn right along with me. I'll ask the questions I imagine you would ask, if you had the chance to sit down with these two guys. You'll see me restructure my framework. You'll see me create a solid financial picture that is possible, workable, and hopeful. You'll see me work together as a team with my husband as we lay a foundation for our future—a future that includes education for our children, a larger home, and all the other things we need, things that up until now have seemed impossible. You can even follow my progress after you've finished reading the book by visiting www.milliondollardiva.com, where I'll be posting updates and sharing new thoughts and ideas about my journey (through the jungle . . . and as I stop to smell the beautiful flowers along the way.

You don't have to be dumb to get into debt. But you also don't have to be a genius to get out of it. I'm going to leave the genius up to Brett and Ethan, and I'll be the willing, and grateful, guinea pig.

Chapter 3

THE MILLION DOLLAR DIVA BLUEPRINT

"Tristi, something completely rocked my world," Ethan said. "A close relative of mine destroyed his entire family. After selling his home at the height of the real-estate boom, he moved to a rural town and bought his next house debt free. Life seemed smooth sailing—all his debts were paid off, and only one more child lived at home. What could go wrong? Everything. Within five years, he lost his home, wife, and entire family. He took the equity in his home and bet it playing options. He lost it all.

"It makes me sick to think about it. His actions were atrocious. But what causes me just as much pain is that his wife didn't have a clue. She even signed off on the loan to allow him access to the money, yet she didn't keep track of what happened to that money.

"I understand the importance of having trust in a marriage, but absolute trust only happens when both partners are on the same page. Today, women must be a part of making the money decisions in their households, and it's not that hard if you have the right ingredients. Whether a woman is single, married, or divorced, she can start the process to become a Million Dollar Diva."

"A Million Dollar Diva?" I asked. "What's that?"

"A diva, in the most positive sense, is a woman— single or married—who is strong and confident," Brett said. "She has focus and direction. She knows what's going on, and she's in control of her life. A Million Dollar Diva is financially savvy and has an exciting plan for her future. She'll ultimately even become a millionaire, safely and securely, and she will have a lot of fun along the way."

I nodded. I definitely want to be more financially savvy, and the idea of having goals, a workable plan, and steps I can take to get me where I want to be, is comforting. I think I've made a lot of decisions because I didn't know what all my options were— in fact, I think a lot of us are that way. We take the conventional wisdom we've been given and do the best we can with it. But we don't realize that there may be new ways to do things, different ways to approach our challenges, that will be far more effective than what we've been trying.

Brett added, "Becoming a Million Dollar Diva happens in three simple stages:

1. Taking ownership
2. Living the proven wealth process
3. Having a "Dream Scene" to keep you on track

"The first step is to come to grips with your situation and take ownership of your future. There are other traits and behaviors we'd like to see you develop as we go through this process with us. Some of them, like confidence, you'll attain as you become better educated about how money works. Others, like goal setting and making smart money decisions, will be the result of the process. However, first you need to change your mind-set to one of empowerment. You're not helpless to solve your problems. In fact, you and your husband are the only ones with that power. Once you fully recognize that, get plugged into the system, and make the right choices, you'll find that you have power you never thought possible."

"People often give their power away unintentionally," Ethan said. "They let other people make their choices for them, and then complain about their situation. They don't get paid enough, things are too expensive, they can't 'afford' to do or buy things. We make *ourselves* helpless—other people don't do that for us. When you're a Million Dollar Diva, you take control of your life! There will always be things we can't control—like the actions of others—but we control ourselves, and we control our reactions to the things other people do. That's where this will benefit you the most—showing you how to take control of your situation and how to act instead of just reacting to the world around you."

I've never been the kind of person who likes giving my power to someone else, and everything Brett and Ethan were describing was exactly what I wanted for myself. I had tried to take control of our family's finances in the past, and I'd do well for a short amount of time, but then they would fight back and take control of me. My husband and I would sit down together, look over the bank statements and our ledger, and be unable to figure out just why it was that we were always in the hole, when—logically—we made enough money. My hope was that I'd learn the vital missing steps while going through this process.

"Every time I turn around, there's another money expert with their own set of ideas for how to handle finances," I said. "How can I get the right education with all these conflicting opinions?"

"Let me break that down for you." Ethan leaned forward. "It begins with how you look at things. We live in a world that is constantly changing—however, true principles never change. True wealth principles that were true a hundred years ago are true today, and will be true a hundred years from now.

"For example, one of these principles is paying yourself first. You will never be able to save for the future and achieve your financial dreams if you don't obey this simple principle. It's as true today as it was one hundred years ago."

"I know we haven't talked about this yet, but how do I pay myself first when I don't have enough to go around?" I asked.

"We'll explain that to you, so just hang in there. I think you'll find it pretty exciting. The second important step is to take advice only from those who teach and *follow* those true wealth principles. Much of it is just common sense. You'll be amazed at the empowering confidence you'll feel when living by those principles."

"Confidence in myself, or in the system?" I asked.

"Both. The confidence in yourself will come as you start living what you are learning and you see the results of your smart money choices, which is the last phase of the formula. The results will come as certainly as the sun rises each morning. No more guessing, wondering, or fear. This will eliminate the doubt or confusion most people feel about their financial situation. Gaining the confidence to take action comes through education."

"I have never really thought about being confident when it comes to money choices. I've always just paid the bills, bought the groceries, and worried if there wasn't money to do more than that. I've been pretty timid about my money in the past."

"When it comes to money, you don't want to be timid," Brett explained. "Being timid can keep you from making the choices you should make, like proper investments that can build your future. Rather than being timid, we recommend being cautiously smart. You definitely want to be careful with your money, and let me get on my soap box for a minute—please don't listen to the gurus on TV who get paid to promote mutual funds. Just stick with the principles of success, which we'll talk about together. Getting wealthy isn't that complicated, if you just follow the steps."

"Okay." I nodded. "I'm just worried that it will be easy to get started, but hard to stay focused— like trying a new diet for a few days, and then giving up."

"That's a problem many people have, and one I had to overcome as well," Ethan said. "Becoming a Million Dollar Diva is a process, and it doesn't happen overnight. Most diet plans don't work because they require people to make drastic changes in a short period of time—and those changes don't stick. The same goes with money. You can see huge improvements in a short period of time, but your overall success comes from having the momentum to keep following the process we're laying out for you until the day you actually become a millionaire and a full-fledged Million Dollar Diva.

"Sadly, we see people all the time who have given up. They feel that their financial problems are too overwhelming, that they'll never get out of their ditches, and that they will never be able to have any of the nicer things in life. They defeat themselves with their attitudes. However—and I can't overstate this—if you follow proven principles, if you have a dream or goal—something important to you that you are really trying to achieve—you will create an atmosphere where it becomes reality."

"Let's go through a critical exercise to providing you the staying power on the Million Dollar Diva journey. If you had all the money you need, and you never had to work again, what would your perfect day look like?" Brett asked. "Let me share mine with you so you can get a feel for what I'm after —I'm at Lake Mead, soaking in the sun on the back deck of my Air Nautique 212 Crossover waterski and wakeboard boat. The speakers on the wakeboard tower are playing James Taylor. The air temperature is 101º, and the water temperature is 81º. I'm wearing the white board shorts I bought in Hawaii, and my wife and three kiddos are playing in the water. Ethan, how about you?"

"I'm at my beach house in Hawaii," Ethan said. "Each morning, I wake up and have breakfast with my family overlooking the grandeur of the ocean. After breakfast, I jump over the rail and play catch with my three kids in the water. We build a sand castle and watch the waves slowly wash it away. In the afternoon, I work on projects that interest me and truly help others. Tristi, what do you want?"

"I feel a little out of the loop—my dreams actually don't include Hawaii. But I want a nice home and all the time I need to write," I said. "I'd like to take some vacations, maybe travel to Paris and draft out a novel while I'm there. I want to spend quality time with my family, and not worry about finances constantly."

"It's okay if Hawaii's not your dream," Brett said. "Paris is nice, too. The important thing is that you have a specific, vivid Dream Scene, like we've just described, whatever it might be. If you don't, you'll find it much harder to stay on the path. Dreams should be what inspire us, what make us get out of bed every morning, what keep us moving toward our goals. They should bring a smile to our faces when we think about them, and keep us from becoming bogged down with the false ideas of 'I can't' or 'I don't deserve.' Dreams are what give us our direction. Without them, there's no value to anything we'll talk about together because you'll have no motivation to take action."

I nodded. This all sounded very familiar to me—I've done a lot of reading about goal setting and dream building, and even attended seminars on it. One of the things I learned is that the human brain can't tell the difference between fantasy and reality. If you take the time to imagine your Dream Scene, as Brett called it, complete with your wardrobe, your menu, and all the things you'll see and experience, your brain will accept all this data as truth. The mind is a goal-seeking mechanism, so it's constantly, but subconsciously, working toward the goal you implant there. By visualizing your dream, you'll find it much easier to make it come to pass in your life.

Our brains often work against us, telling us we can't have what we most want because we feed it negativity. The world is a *very* negative place—the news, TV shows about murder and crime, and the horrible things people do to one another. By default, our thoughts often slide into the slums of negativity. We're reminded of all the times in the past when we tried and failed. We remember that embarrassing moment when we totally tanked right in the middle of a presentation and ended up losing the account. We replay that scene endlessly in our minds.

But if we feed our brains a vivid scene of success, happiness, and images of what we want to achieve in our lives, we are in a better position to receive the things we most want. I shared this with Brett and Ethan.

"We've seen this over and over again, and it's more than just the 'positive thinking' stuff we've heard for years," Brett said. "It's actually a scientifically proven fact that the more specific, clear, and vivid you can make your Dream Scene in your mind, the more likely you will be to achieve it. That's why we encourage everyone we work with to start with a dream. Most people's dreams are broken. They can't think beyond this week's check and paying the bills, let alone a life of freedom, happiness, and wealth. This obviously isn't working well for most people because they keep getting the same results.

"As a Million Dollar Diva, you'll become an expert when it comes to dreaming. You'll have your goals cemented in your mind, and you'll have a white-hot burning desire to achieve them. This white-hot desire is the final ingredient. It's the momentum that will keep you successfully on the path. You'll have good and bad days, but every morning you'll wake up with the energy to keep going. You'll have the ultimate confidence that you can arrive because you've taken ownership of the situation, properly educated yourself, and started making good money decisions."

* * *

Brett and Ethan asked me some important questions to help me create my Dream Scene, and I think it will be helpful for you to go through the exercise as well. Take out a paper and pen, or write them here in the book (go ahead . . . it's your book). Answer these quick questions, and if you're married, have your husband go through this exercise, too, so you can imagine your dreams together.

If you had all the money you needed, and you never had to work again, what would your perfect day look like?

- Who's there with you?
- What does the air feel like?
- What does it smell like?

Add some details—can you feel the sun on your face, or the sand beneath your toes, or see the faces of the people around you?

How do you feel about life—are you fulfilled? Excited? Alive?

This is power. Dreams drive action. Playing out this Dream Scene each day will give you the energy you need to succeed—and to help you truly become a strong, vital Million Dollar Diva.

Chapter 4

I Could Just Scream!

Writing this book about finances hasn't proven to be the easiest thing I've ever done. Yes, I'm a published author and editor—writing itself isn't new to me. But the financial part *is* new, and I have to admit, my emotions are getting dragged into this a little more than I would like.

A little background on me—I mentioned already that I grew up . . . not *poor*, exactly, but without a lot of things I would have liked to have, and to be honest, some things I needed. I have memories of our heat, electricity, and phone being shut off, turned on again later, only to be shut off again. New clothes didn't happen very often, and the food in the house was sometimes in short supply. As a child, I didn't know how to define what I was feeling, but as an adult, I can label it properly: I didn't feel secure. And security is a big deal when you're talking about money—especially, I learned from talking with friends, for women.

Traditionally, women have relied on men for their support. They were provided for by their fathers during childhood, and then their care and keeping was turned over to their husbands. In the past, it's even been somewhat of a cultural taboo for women to talk about finances, or to be present when money is discussed.

Even though things have changed in our society, and women now have the ability and are encouraged to get jobs and support themselves, as children they are still dependent on others to take care of them, and security can be a big issue. For women who are dependent on husbands for their support, these feelings can continue into their adulthood. For me, as a stay-at-home mom, it's a very big deal because all the money issues I currently face tie me right back to those feelings I had as a child. I can sit here and tell myself I'm not five anymore, but every time I see that bank balance dip below a certain number, I *feel* five again, and feelings will trump logic every time.

Emotions create a physical reaction in our bodies. I pointed this out in a writing class I taught not long ago—when we feel an emotion, we don't just feel sad or lonely or scared. We have physical reactions that go along with it. Our hands might get clammy when we're nervous. Our stomach might clench when we get scared. We might not be conscious of those physical reactions when they happen, but we do need to become aware of them. They can dictate our actions, how we deal with the emotions. We might even find our personalities changing when we're faced with a sudden, huge emotion—think about how you'd react if someone broke into your home. You might not ordinarily be an aggressive person, but you'd do whatever you could to protect your family, right?

When it comes to money, do you ever feel afraid? I know I do. And sometimes that emotion, and its very unpleasant physical counterparts, make me act irrationally. Out of fear, I might not make a wise investment, or I might make a purchase that I think is going to help me, but in the long run, will hurt me. If I'm feeling sad or lonely, I might buy something in the hopes that it will cheer me up. But it doesn't, because I'm not dealing with the key emotion. And you know what . . . I didn't enjoy using that item because I felt guilty about it.

Money is an instrument of change—we need money if we want to move, for instance, and sometimes our lack of finances can make us feel trapped and unable to progress. We can feel claustrophobic, helpless, and desperate—all emotions that can lead us to make unwise decisions.

Sometimes we think we're not good mothers if we don't spend a lot of money on our children. We fear we're depriving them, that they won't feel as loved, or that they'll do without something they really need. Believe me—I've been there.

Financial success can also impact our feelings of personal success. If we don't make as much money as Susan or Barbara, we feel slightly inferior. Or maybe Kate's husband just got a big raise, and your husband didn't. We can feel as though we're not as deserving, talented, or appreciated, and these emotions wreak havoc on our internal peace and the way in which we view the world.

We sometimes buy things because we envy what someone else has, or because we want revenge, or because we like the way we feel when we shop—it really is an endorphin high. Chemicals are released into our blood streams that literally change our bodies and affect how we make decisions. It's an eye-opening experience when people realize that money isn't really about math and numbers at all—it's about emotions! Money is emotional, not logical or financial, and that's why it's so hard to control. The goals, the good intentions, the New Year's resolutions to get out of debt—the list could go on and on. We all want to get under financial control, yet it's extremely difficult to do.

I asked Brett his thoughts on this.

"Have you ever gotten mad at your husband or kids, and you knew you shouldn't lose your temper, but you yelled and screamed anyway?" he asked. "If you're human, you probably know what I'm talking about."

"I am human, but I don't want to admit anything," I replied.

"Well, when we get emotional, it's hard to control our actions. Emotions are extremely powerful. They give us the ability to do things we wouldn't normally be able to do. This is a perfect example of why it's so hard to control our spending, or save money for a rainy day, because it's like trying to control our temper."

"So, how *do* I control my financial emotions, then?"

Brett responded, "The single most important thing you can do is to track your spending. My mentor, Peter, taught me years ago, 'When you track it, you control it.' This is true of your spending, but it also relates to any area of your life in which you want to make a change. My wife just had our third child, and she's working very hard to lose the baby weight. She told me the other day, 'When I write down what I've eaten, it's a lot easier for me to control what I eat. When I don't track it, I just munch on a little of this and a little of that, and before I know it, I've eaten way more calories than I even realize.'

"I agreed, and told her we share the same concepts with our clients who are trying to get their finances back on track. If you don't track what you spend, it's easy to spend a little here and a little there, and before you know it, those twenty dollar purchases at the store or out to dinner add up to a lot more than we thought."

I nodded. "I've noticed that, too. I've also noticed the emotional connection, and I think my two biggest emotions are fear and fear. That is to say, fear of the unknown and fear of running out. I worry that I don't know where our money will come from, and I worry that when it does come, it won't be enough."

"Fear can paralyze us from taking action, or it can catalyze us into making the changes we need for our growth. And I understand that fear," Brett answered. "I've owned my own business for the past decade during some of the worst times in the past century—the market crashes after 9/11 and the more recent recession. I've felt the fear of not being able to provide for my family. It's a sickening, haunting feeling that eats away at you, and never leaves you.

"Throughout this process, I will show you the most effective way I've ever found to combat the fear—or reality—of not having enough money. Right now, let's talk about controlling the emotions that drive people to spend money they don't have, to get deeply into debt, and to carry extreme guilt for spending more than they should.

"There are few things in this life that are more devastating to the personal psyche and to a family dynamic than debt. It's an albatross hanging around your neck. It's a constant reminder of the decisions you wish you hadn't made, like a mirror on the wall exposing your ugliest blemishes and making many of us feel like losers. We feel like we're inferior because we lack self-control, and ultimately it can destroy self-esteem.

"This is something most people don't talk about. But once your self-esteem is crushed, it's very difficult to maintain a good marriage or be a good parent because it's difficult to love others if we don't love ourselves."

"I've noticed that," I replied. "When I'm carrying around financial baggage, it's hard to feel good about myself, or to think about anything else. So tell me what to do about it."

"There are a few simple steps that can stop this 'emotional spending' problem dead in its tracks. Just remember . . . when you track it, you control it. Now let's take a couple of those steps together.

"Get out some paper and write down how you feel when you are about to buy something you really want. How do you feel when you go out to dinner at a nice restaurant, but you know you can't afford it, so it's going on the credit card? See if you can identify what emotion is driving you to make that decision. Write down how you feel when a friend shops with no conscience, but you can't because you are worried about money. Write down how you feel when you look at the credit card statements or at any of your other loans.

"Now write down how you feel, or how you imagine you'd feel, if you were completely out of debt, including your house. How would you feel the day the title showed up in the mail box? Imagine what it would feel like to have no debt on your cars, either. No one will see this but you, so don't feel embarrassed to write down everything that comes to mind. Then write down *when* you feel strong emotions, both positive and negative. For instance, you might feel afraid while you're paying the bills, and you might feel relief when you're done.

"Next, take a look at the emotions that are driving you to spend money. Why are you doing it? Being truthful with yourself here will go a long way toward controlling your emotions the next time you are in that situation.

"Lastly, if you do nothing else, do this one thing. Track your spending. Every dollar, whether it's cash or credit, or debit or gift card. I recommend using a Smartphone app, and have listed several free apps at www.milliondollardiva.com. Most people are never going to take the time to write something down when they get home, but most of us have our phones with us all the time and can quickly enter the information into the app. And make sure you write down the expense immediately. Don't let it go until the end of the day. It's easy to forget at that point. This is so important that I'd say it's worth getting a Smartphone phone *just* for this purpose. It will make such a profound difference in your life. If you don't have a Smartphone, you can still track spending with a simple ledger or Excel spreadsheet.

"When you establish your spending plan for the month, you know you'll have, say, $550 for food, gas, and entertainment. If you see by the 15th of the month that you have already spent $450, you know you need to cut way back, not go out to eat, and ration your dinero for the next two weeks. Having this information is *incredibly* empowering. You know how much you have left, so it's easy to plan accordingly and not get yourself into debt. If you don't know how much you've spent, it's easy to just keep on spending, thinking that twenty bucks here and forty bucks there isn't too much. But it adds up more quickly than any of us think at the time. On the positive side, if you get to the end of the month and you have an extra $50 you haven't spent, it's fun to go out and do whatever you want with it. Go shopping, go out to dinner and a movie, and never feel guilty about it . . . because it's part of the plan."

"I love that idea," I said. "But I wonder if I could ask you another question. This one's a little more personal. My biggest emotional problems in regards to money go back to my childhood, when I didn't have enough. Today, when I'm faced with a bill I don't know how to pay, or we're running out of food money, it hits my sense of security, and I overreact. I get a little bit panicky. How do I deal with that?"

"It's important to remember that you're not a child anymore," Brett said. "You are in control of your life, and you can deal with those emotions from a mature standpoint. When they arise, don't smother them—allow yourself to feel them. Writing it all out in a journal might be useful. Acknowledge that you went through a tough time, but then realize that you're in the driver's seat now. You have choices, you have options, and you can find ways to overcome your problems. As we work through this program, we'll show you ways to increase your income so hopefully you won't find yourself in that situation again. But if you do, you'll have the tools to deal with it."

Brett stood up and went to the whiteboard in his office. He drew out a circle and put lines through it, making it look like a bicycle tire.

"I call this the circle of life. These sections represent the different areas in our lives— emotional, spiritual, health, social, financial, and relationships. Self-help gurus will tell you that you have to be in balance in all these areas for a happy life. But they're wrong."

"What do you mean?" I asked.

"What happens if you don't do your sit-ups for the next thirty days? Are you going to die of a heart attack as a result of neglect?" Brett asked, pointing to the health slice of the pie.

"Probably not," I replied.

"On the spiritual side, what if you don't say your prayers for a month straight . . . are you going to end up in hell?"

"I hope not," I said, laughing. "I guess it depends on what else I was doing during those thirty days."

"What if you don't call your friends for a couple of weeks—is your world going to come to a screeching halt? Of course not. And if you don't get in touch with your inner child and talk out all your emotional problems for a month or two, you'll still probably be able to function as a human being, right?

"But let me ask you this . . . what happens if the average person doesn't have any money for an entire month?"

"That's a problem." Just imagining it made me feel a little tense, even though I knew it was a pretend scenario.

"It's a *big* problem. Kids going hungry, house payments missed, no gas to get to work, potential of losing your job for not showing up, no money to pay electric bills, and you can see where I'm going with this.

"Now don't misunderstand—I'm not saying that money is the most important part of your life, but lack of money has the most immediate impact on your life."

I nodded. "Yeah, I see that."

"That's why it's critical that you get this right. We're talking about families being torn apart, marriages destroyed, and lives ruined *all the time* because people don't get this. I can't express it strongly enough . . . we've got to win the money game."

Brett drew a new picture on the board, this time with a dollar sign in the middle of the pie. "Do you see how all the other slices of the pie are now connected to the money? That's how it really is, and you need to view it that way."

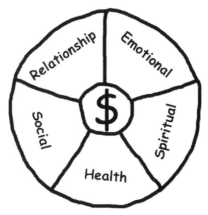

"That also explains why money is so emotional—because everything else hinges on it," I said, studying the board.

"Exactly. Money isn't everything, but everything is connected to it. We may not like it, but that's how it is. And once we understand that, we have control of it, and we can make it work for us."

That made so much sense to me. You can't fight an enemy you don't understand.

I have hated money my whole life. I've resented it, fought against it, and even considered moving to an island where everyone trades shells instead. But after having this talk with Brett, I realized that money wasn't the problem—it's the attitudes people have about money that's the problem. Whether it's greed, whether it's jealousy or fear or even generosity and goodwill—people's attitudes are what make money what it is, and I don't have to let money control me. I can control it . . . and having that knowledge feels really good.

Chapter 5

THE WOMAN IN THE MIRROR

My husband and I had both been working long hours, doing everything we could to try to pay off our debts and get into a larger home, but a solution to our problems just didn't seem any closer. I tossed some ideas back and forth with my husband, and neither of us felt particularly good about anything that came to mind. Bankruptcy isn't something we've ever considered—we feel that as we got ourselves into debt, we should get ourselves out of it. We both believe in paying our own way.

As I prepared to meet with Brett and Ethan to discuss our family finances, I was a little nervous. Showing someone your finances is like pulling the Band-Aid off your ugly scab and showing it off. It's worse than that, though—it's showing the scab of a wound you inflicted upon yourself.

But it's got to hurt in order to heal.

In thinking about our situation, I wondered if we could find a good debt consolidation company, one that would help us pay off our bills without ruining our credit, and that would help us feel as though we were taking charge of our debt instead of running away from it. This was one of the first questions I asked Brett and Ethan.

"Many of the credit-repair companies out there are actually running scams and don't do what they say they will," Ethan told me. "In addition, they might say they won't ruin your credit, but chances are, they will. There are *some* good debt consolidation companies, though, and we can help you find one, if that's the direction you decide to go."

"What we'd like to do first is get a better idea of your situation," Brett said. "We have some special debt analysis software that will chart out all your bills and help you get *yourself* consolidated. Once you see where you are, then you can start making plans for how to take the next step. We also have a chart that will help you map out your expenditures."

That sounded great—I'm the kind of person who likes to see things laid out in front of me. It also made me a little bit nervous. I knew I was going to see things I wouldn't like.

"We want to help people take ownership of their situation," Brett continued. "It gives them a feeling of empowerment. Far too many people feel entitled, and that's a trap. It's slavery. Once a person takes ownership of their situation, they have the power to change it."

Brett e-mailed to me the Drive Down debt analysis software and the expense tracking sheet. When they arrived in my inbox, I was excited—here were the tools I would need to start really getting a handle on things.

I signed in to the Drive Down debt online software with my e-mail address and a password I created, and then I went through and filled out the form. I put in the name of the debtor, the reason for the debt (okay, that part opened my eyes quite a lot), and then the interest rate and the monthly payment. It took me a few minutes to locate some of this information. Have you ever noticed how credit card bills sort of tuck the interest rate away where you can't see it, and you have to read through to page four of the document in order to learn how much you're forking over in extra charges? I was able to save my progress and come back to the site, though, which was nice—I didn't have to do the whole thing in one sitting.

The software then calculated how much money I would end up giving those debtors before I was done, and it told me how many more months I would be paying on those debts. That was a humbling experience. But as I was going through it, I remembered what Brett had said—"If you track it, you control it." I didn't want to continue to be lost in the fog of ignorance, knowing we had financial problems but not defining them. I would rather know what I was facing.

And what *was* I facing? My husband and I would be paying almost $20,000 in interest by the time we got those debts paid off, and some of them wouldn't be paid in full for years.

When I was done, I e-mailed the reports to Brett and Ethan. The software is set up in such a way that they can't just go in there and look at it for themselves, which made me feel more secure about the process. They wouldn't know anything I didn't choose to tell them. The software hadn't asked me for any credit card numbers or any other personal information, and I appreciated the level of privacy I was afforded.

After I e-mailed over the reports, I met with Brett to discuss what they meant.

"As I look at your Wealth Builder printout and your true debt picture, I'd like to ask you, how was it, going through this process? Was it difficult, sickening, exciting—how did it make you feel?" Brett asked.

I laughed. Honestly, it was probably a little bit of all of the above. "We've always tried to keep tabs on our debt situation, but we haven't known what to do about it. So there weren't any surprises, really, except for one thing—the way the interest adds up. I hadn't realized how much interest we were paying on our debts—almost $20,000 by the time it's all paid off."

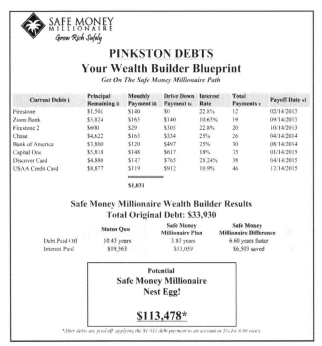

"As you look at the software, you can see that it organizes the debts in the order they'll be paid off. The gurus always tell you to target the debts with the highest interest rates first, but over and over, we've seen that if you focus on the one that will be paid off the soonest according to the calendar, you've freed up money to use in paying down the next debt. Your Firestone bill has only twelve payments until it's all paid off. This means that in one year's time, you'll have an extra $140 dollars to pay down the next debt."

"Instead of spending it on something else."

"Exactly. Every time we pay off a debt, we're going to use that money to 'drive down' the next debt—that's where the name Drive Down comes from. So as you look at your chart, our next goal is to pay off Zions Bank. But we're no longer just paying them $165. We're paying them $165 plus $140. After that debt is paid off—which is sooner than it was before—we roll that money down to pay off the next Firestone bill. You have two accounts with them?"

"Yes. We had some emergency car repairs that the first account couldn't handle."

"Okay, so we'll pay off the second Firestone card next. Just follow the chart all the way to the bottom, and you'll see some interesting things. First of all, your entire debt load will be paid off in 3.83 years, instead of the 10.43 years it would take if you didn't roll your money over. And look how much interest you'd be saving."

I blinked. "I'd be saving over $6,500 dollars in interest."

"That's right, and you're doing this using the money you're *already* spending on your debts. You're just driving it down instead of letting that money get absorbed back into your spending."

"That's pretty awesome."

"Now look down at the bottom of the sheet. See where it says 'Safe Money Millionaire Nest Egg'? When your debts are paid off, if you take the money you would have been spending on your bills and place it in an account that will generate 5% interest, you could create a nest egg of over $113,000 dollars. All that just by using the money you're already spending, but in a wiser way."

"So by the time I reach retirement age, I'd have over $113,000?" That sounded pretty good to me.

"No. This is by the time you would have paid off your debt originally."

"What?" I looked at the chart. "You mean that in 10.43 years, I could have $113,000 dollars? And I'd be out of debt?"

"Yes. That's if you placed the money in an account that was getting 5%, which is really simple to do."

"Wow. That's amazing." I'd heard this principle before, rolling your money over to your next debt, but every time I'd tried it in the past, there was always another use for that freed-up cash. I could tell this would take some focus and commitment, but seeing that nest egg number at the bottom was certainly a good incentive to give it a better try.

"Now let's take this a step further," Brett continued. "What if you were to find another $50 somewhere in your budget, and you applied that toward your first debt, making your payment $190 per month instead of $140? You'd have Firestone paid off in nine months instead of twelve, and then you could roll that $190 down to the next debt. By following the chart down to the bottom, you'd get out of debt in 3.67 years, and you'd save

$6,942 in interest. And then check it out—if you took that money and saved it in a 5% interest account, you'd have a nest egg of $123,000 dollars in ten years."

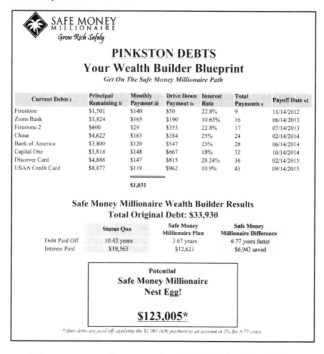

"I'm not sure how to find $50," I said. "Things are really tight right now."

"In just a few minutes, I'll show you some ways to find money in your budget. Right now, I'd like to focus on the possibilities. How do you feel about this?" Brett pointed to the chart that showed the extra $50 added to the mix.

"It feels hopeful. Like there's something we can really do about our situation."

"Great. Now let me show you another chart."

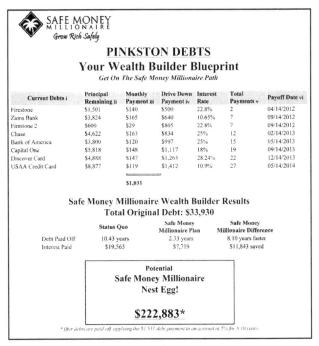

Safe Money Millionaire Wealth Builder Results

	Status Quo	Safe Money Millionaire Plan	Safe Money Millionaire Difference
Debt Paid Off	10.43 years	2.33 years	8.10 years faster
Interest Paid	$19,563	$7,719	$11,843 saved

"Let's say you were able to take your business to a new level, and you added $500 to your Drive Down payment. Your Firestone bill would be gone in two months, and you'd have $640 to roll over to the next debt. By following this chart, you'd have all your debts paid off in 2.33 years, and you would save over $11,000 in interest. And check out this nest egg. If you put your money in an account getting 5%, you would have $222,883 at the end of ten years."

"That's really significant," I said. "Thanks for breaking this down for me—I like seeing all these possibilities for the first time. I also like knowing that even if I can't find an extra $50, I can still work the program and make definite headway."

"You'll absolutely make headway, but don't give up on that $50," Brett said. "I have some ideas already, just by looking over your finances. Now, I noticed you don't have a house payment."

"That's right. We own a trailer home, and we just make a monthly rent payment for the land."

"I'd like to show you a sample chart we made to illustrate how this system would work for a homeowner." Brett showed me this page:

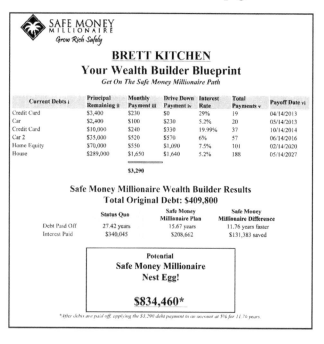

SAFE MONEY MILLIONAIRE
Grow Rich Safely

BRETT KITCHEN
Your Wealth Builder Blueprint
Get On The Safe Money Millionaire Path

Current Debts i	Principal Remaining ii	Monthly Payment iii	Drive Down Payment iv	Interest Rate	Total Payments v	Payoff Date vi
Credit Card	$3,400	$230	$0	29%	19	04/14/2013
Car	$2,400	$100	$230	5.2%	20	05/14/2013
Credit Card	$10,000	$240	$330	19.99%	37	10/14/2014
Car 2	$35,000	$520	$570	6%	57	06/14/2016
Home Equity	$70,000	$550	$1,090	7.5%	101	02/14/2020
House	$289,000	$1,650	$1,640	5.2%	188	05/14/2027

$3,290

Safe Money Millionaire Wealth Builder Results
Total Original Debt: $409,800

	Status Quo	Safe Money Millionaire Plan	Safe Money Millionaire Difference
Debt Paid Off	27.42 years	15.67 years	11.76 years faster
Interest Paid	$340,045	$208,662	$131,383 saved

**Potential
Safe Money Millionaire
Nest Egg!**

$834,460*

After debts are paid off, applying the $3,290 debt payment to an account at 5% for 11.76 years.

"This shows a person who has a house payment, two car payments, and a couple of credit cards—pretty typical of today's homeowner. Just by following this simple formula and rolling his money into the next debt, he would get out of debt eleven years faster, and he'd have a nest egg of over $800,000."

"Wow. That's amazing."

"What's amazing is the power people have to change their circumstances without even realizing it. Did you know you could put aside that much money in just ten years?"

"I had no idea. I'm a little mind-boggled right now, to be honest, and it all looks so easy."

"It is easy," Brett told me. "It takes some concentration and dedication, but it's a really simple plan to follow. Now, are you ready to find that fifty dollars in your budget?"

"Absolutely." I had been looking for extra money—any extra money—for a while, and hadn't found any. I couldn't wait to hear what Brett could do for me.

Visit:

www.milliondollardiva.com

to create your own Drive Down Debt report,

and see how quickly you can be

completely out of debt.

Chapter 6

OWNERSHIP
OR ENTITLEMENT?

"So I bet you're excited to find that fifty dollars," Brett said.

"Yeah, I thought that's what we were doing next."

"We'll get to that, but we feel we can't go further until we've discussed something very important with you, a fundamental truth that will determine your success or failure. It's rare that you can point to one single thing that holds this kind of power, but in this case, you really can. This principle will change everything for you.

"I started learning it when I was six years old. I was sitting in Sunday School, and Blake, a boy who lived one street over from me, punched me. I started crying because I was a wimpy little six-year-old. The teacher took me and Blake out of the room and asked what was going on. She sent for my parents, and Blake's parents, too. I told them Blake had punched me in the stomach. In reality, he'd punched me a little lower, but I was too embarrassed to admit that.

"Blake's parents started blaming me, asking what I'd done to him. What happened next really affected my life and his life forever, and it was a defining moment for us both. It foreshadowed how our lives would go from that moment forward. Blake's parents were focused on finding out what I'd done to provoke him—they never asked Blake why he'd done it.

"My parents, on the other hand, asked me what happened. I explained that he was being mean and had punched me. I don't actually remember why he had done it, but I remember how his parents reacted. They hugged him, told him it wasn't his fault, and that everything was going to be okay. He punched me for no reason, his parents didn't give him any discipline or responsibility for what happened, and that turned out to be a pattern he'd follow his whole life."

"I feel sorry for him," I said. "What did your parents say to you about it?"

"My dad pulled me aside and said, 'Brett, when you get hit like that, it's not always okay to start crying. You need to fight back, you need to defend yourself. Someone's not always going to be there to bail you out.' We know a lot about bailouts in this country, don't we? My dad taught me when I was six years old that you can't depend on somebody else to bail you out—you'd better learn how to fight back.

"In fact, he told me a story of how his dad had paid him a quarter for every fight he got into as a kid, so he could learn to be tough. My dad didn't do that for me, but he taught me that I need to take ownership for my life and not depend on somebody else to help me out of my difficulties. It was an important realization for me to make. If I wanted to buy something, I needed to earn the money myself. In fact, I never dared ask my dad for money because I already knew what he would say. The only time we'd ever go to a restaurant or a fast-food place was when we were on vacation. We would go to McDonald's or Wendy's. But we could never order a combo meal. We could get a sandwich and maybe some French fries, if we were lucky. But we'd never order a milkshake or a soda or anything like that. We'd just be shot down immediately. Dad would tell us we could only get a shake if we paid for it ourselves.

"So from my youngest years, I knew that I had to work for the things I wanted. My dad was all about hard work, about ownership—not entitlements or handouts. And so we, obviously, had to earn our keep around the house. Every day when I got home from school, I had a list of chores a mile long. I still hate the word 'chores' to this day.

"On Saturdays, Dad would take us down to his manufacturing plant, and we would clean the bathroom. If you've ever been to a manufacturing plant, you know it's a dirty place, and the bathrooms were disgusting. The toilets were black and greasy. So were the sinks. And the paper towel towers were so tall that if they fell over, it was like you'd get smothered to death. We'd take a big bag into the bathrooms and stuff all the paper towels into it, and we'd get twenty-five cents per bathroom we cleaned. My dad worked hard, and he taught us to work hard.

"He started the manufacturing company when we were in the middle of the Carter years—15% inflation, 15% interest rates, and high unemployment. My parents were living in a garage that had been converted into a studio apartment, and they lived a very difficult life. But I learned as a kid not to expect a handout from anyone, and the things they taught me have been absolutely critical to me throughout my life. I put myself through college. I worked hard to earn scholarships and to keep jobs while at school. And this made me value the education I was getting."

"I bet it did," I replied. "I've noticed that people tend to appreciate the things they've worked hard to get."

"It's true. And when I started my first company, I'd be up all night working to get stuff done so my company would stay afloat. Then for breakfast I'd get a Dr. Pepper to keep me awake for the next workday. And what are the fruits of the lessons I've been taught? Ethan and I have built two million-dollar companies. We've been featured on Inc.

Magazine's bestseller list for our most recent book, *Safe Money Millionaire*. We built one of our companies during the heart of the deepest recession since the Great Depression. Things like that don't happen if you're just sitting around, waiting for a handout."

"No, they don't," I agreed.

"I also have three beautiful children, a beautiful wife, and a very happy life. I thank my parents for what they taught me." Brett leaned forward. "About six years ago, the day my first son was born, I heard some news about my friend Blake who had punched me all those years ago. His story didn't turn out so well."

"Oh, yeah?" I had wondered about that . . .

"Let me backtrack a little bit. As I continued to hang out with Blake when I was younger, I would hear him talk back to his mother and even tell her to shut up at times. And I just couldn't believe it. I mean, if that ever happened in my house, I would've been smacked hard and sent to my room for life without parole. I guarantee it. And any time Blake wanted something, he would just tell his mom to get it for him. It wasn't even like he was asking for it—he was giving orders. Whether it was a bike or a video game or something to do with his new tree house or toys or money to go out and do whatever he wanted, he would get whatever he asked for. He was actually the one who taught me how to steal."

"You little thief," I teased.

"Yeah, I'm not really proud of that, and my mom and I went back to the store and made things right. As Blake and I got older, I distanced myself from him because he was getting worse and worse. He was doing drugs, and stealing, and had problems with the law. He had never learned the value of working for something, of owning something because of his blood, sweat, and tears. He never had to because he was on the Blake entitlement program—he could get whatever he wanted, whenever he wanted. Why go to work if he could get everything for free? That's the way he was raised.

"His parents literally got to a point where they couldn't handle him. They sent him to troubled kid camps to try to fix his behavior. But it was too late."

"That must have been hard on his parents, seeing how he turned out," I commented.

"It really was. And like I mentioned before, on the day my son was born, I heard from a mutual friend that Blake was in jail. Here I was, celebrating one of the greatest days of my life with my wife and family, and Blake was in a cage. Barred up, unable to do anything with his life because of his entitlement upbringing."

"That's really sad," I said. "And to think that to some extent, he didn't know better."

"True—it came from the way he was raised. But he had every chance as an adult to overcome it. That's one of the things Ethan and I most want to fix—the philosophy under which many of the people in this country operate. Entitlement really is like a drug, and it slowly creeps into a person and starts small addictions. As it grows, it gets worse and worse and worse. Ultimately, it robs you of your life and your freedom. But if you're willing to take a stand and say, you know what? I'm not going to rely on anybody else. I'm not going to insist that I deserve something. At that point, you gain freedom and control of your life. And that's when you can really build something powerful for yourself."

Ethan cleared his throat. "It's really devastating to see what drugs do to people. I have a personal friend who lost everything, and he was never able to get off the drugs. He tried to go through rehab, but was unsuccessful. His whole life was like that—he was never able to be consistent with his progress, and he was never happy. He couldn't have a long-term relationship, either.

"I remember a commercial back when I was a kid—they'd crack an egg into a frying pan and say, 'This is your brain on drugs.' Stories like my friend's are the reason why we've had so many anti-drug commercials."

"I saw that commercial, too," I said. "And all the spin-offs people made from it."

Ethan nodded. "My wife's a lawyer who sometimes volunteers her time to help out in the community, and she talked to a police officer who told her that it's almost impossible to get off certain drugs. You have to be a person of tremendous will and determination to make rehab work, or the addiction will destroy your life. There are people just like Blake who get hooked on being entitled, and they can't get off. Once the shackles are on, they're chained, even though it's psychologically. No one is speaking out against the entitlement programs in this country, but they affect us negatively on a core emotional level."

"Exactly," Brett said. "If you can understand the difference between ownership and entitlement, you will have the difference between control and freedom, or chains and disappointment, for the rest of your life. Feelings of entitlement kill ambition. They kill the spirit of creation, of work, of being in control of your life. They make people feel like they deserve something they truly don't deserve.

"Let's go back a few hundred years to the pilgrims who came across the ocean to the United States of America. What did they deserve? Did they deserve time off? Or to make more than minimum wage? Or vacation packages? Or insurance programs if they accidentally got stepped on by one of the horses while they were plowing the fields? They weren't *entitled* to anything—they *worked* for everything they got, and they were better for it. This became a great nation because of it.

"Never before in the history of the world have people lived under such a philosophy of entitlement. You know, one hundred years ago, five hundred years ago, two thousand years ago, people weren't taking vacations and getting paid time off. They woke up and put their noses to the grindstone to stay alive. Not that I envy them—I don't. I love the fact that I can take off and go on vacations and see the wonders of the world. But the question is, are we entitled to it? Do we deserve it? Or do we earn it? Do we own it?

"There are people in the country," Brett continued, "where three generations are living on entitlement programs. It really does ruin their hope and their desire to live. What's interesting is when you look at the drug dealer and the person who's taking the drugs, it's not the drug dealer getting hurt by it—the person taking the drugs is the person who gets hurt. It's the same thing with entitlement. The victims are the people who are receiving it because it robs them of their self-fulfillment and the potential to control their own destiny.

"I read a story online not too long ago, and one of the comments after it just blew me away," Brett said. "I had to copy it down, it was so outrageous. Listen to this:

> *"IT'S TIME WE GET BACK TO REALIZING THAT WE ARE ENTITLED. We're entitled to expect the rich to pay their fair share. We're entitled to unemployment. In fact, we're entitled to an unemployment check when we're unemployed because we've been paying into it our whole lives. No more welfare for the wealthy—we are entitled.'*

"What does this guy gain by looking for a handout? What positive things are going to happen to him when he has this attitude? There's nothing to be gained other than getting something for nothing.

"Now, we're not talking about charity. Let's be clear here—we are believers in charity and in helping people improve their station in life based on the fact that they *can* do something to improve. Entitlement is getting something for nothing and never having to do anything for it."

Ethan nodded. "We believe in programs that help people out. But their whole purpose is to get that person on their feet, right? Bad things can happen to good people. Everyone can have a catastrophic event in their lives. You could lose a lot of money, have a health issue, a death in the family—those things happen, and there are programs to help. But the purpose of those programs is—or should be—to teach you how to get you back on your feet, to be independent again."

"I definitely agree," Brett said. "We're influenced so heavily by the federal government. If you go back over the course of history, you'll see that the more people are dependent upon the government, the more control the government has. Welfare isn't to help people get back on their feet—it's to make them dependent, to take away their power.

"If you want to own the things in your life, it does take a little bit of introspection. It takes looking in the mirror and admitting that you own the circumstances you're in right now, in every segment of your life. When you're honest with yourself, you have the ability to make great strides. When you're lying to yourself, you can't make progress because there's no foundation.

"That's why we wanted to talk to you before we went much further, Tristi. You need to take ownership of your situation, and then take ownership of your ability to change it. Can you do that?"

"Absolutely. And I can absolutely take ownership of my part in changing it—that makes me feel as though I can undo the mistakes of my past and start with a clean slate."

"You can start over again, and we'll show you how to keep from repeating your same mistakes over and over again. It comes right back to ownership—you own your actions, and you will own your success or your failure," Brett said.

"I'd like to share with you a poem I heard some years back by a man named William Ernest Henley. It's called *Invictus*, and it goes like this:

> "'*Out of the night that covers me,*
> *Black as the Pit from pole to pole,*
> *I thank whatever gods may be*
> *For my unconquerable soul.*

In the fell clutch of circumstance
I have not winced nor cried aloud.
Under the bludgeonings of chance
My head is bloody, but not bowed.

Beyond this place of wrath and tears
Looms but the Horror of the shade,
And yet the menace of the years
Finds, and shall find, me unafraid.

It matters not how strait the gate,
How charged with punishments the scroll.
I am the master of my fate:
I am the captain of my soul.'

"I believe that we are all the masters of our fate and the captains of our souls," Brett said. "We can create whatever we want in our lives and improve whatever difficult circumstances we have by taking ownership. Tristi, are you and Matt willing to go on this ride with us? We'll help you learn how we've done it in our own lives, and how we can help you create it for yourselves."

"I'm one hundred percent committed," I replied. "Let's do it."

Chapter 7

GIVING OURSELVES A RAISE

"All right, now we're going to talk about that fifty dollars," Brett said. "Thanks for your patience—but we need to get the principles in place so you can build on the right foundation. And now that we've looked over your debts and created your charts, we have a game plan, or a recipe, to get you out of debt. How are you feeling right now?"

"Really optimistic," I told him. "I'm seeing possibilities I didn't know existed. And I really appreciated how the software did the math for me. It took away all my excuses and created a light at the end of the tunnel."

"Great. And you've had a chance to see that you don't have to be making millions of dollars to make this work—you just have to be making the right decisions with your money. I don't have any magical solutions to make your debts go away, but I'm a true believer in finding money that's currently going to waste and amplifying your income.

"We said we were going to put in an extra $50 a month. That's helpful, but it doesn't make a huge difference. If you found money you're wasting right now and increased your income a bit, you'll be surprised how quickly we'll be able to put $500 a month into the program, and you'll be out of debt in less than three years. That would be worth it, wouldn't it?"

"Absolutely." Less than three years? Yeah, I was definitely listening.

"You need to think creatively to solve your financial problems. As Einstein said, 'Problems cannot be solved by the same level of thinking that created them.' The ideas I'm going to suggest are probably not 'common sense,' but be willing to consider them, because we can see the substantial impact this is going to have on your financial situation.

"Most people don't want to put extra money toward paying off their debt because they don't see in black and white what it's going to do for them. They don't feel that putting an extra $30 on their credit card bill is going to do much good, so they decide to spend it on themselves instead. But when they see the Wealth Builder printout, it changes their perspective, and they start to get it.

"We're going to look at your daily expenses now and see where you may be wasting money without being aware of it. Often I help people find $300, $500, even $1000 or more."

I agreed to go through the process, but I wasn't sure what Brett was going to find. My husband and I had already made the choice to live frugally, and our expenses had been narrowed as far as we knew how to narrow them. We even shut off our cable a few years back—not only because it saves us some money, but because we were frustrated with how much our children fought after watching TV. I was definitely curious to hear what Brett would have to say next.

"Let's get to the fun part—what I call 'giving yourself a raise.'"

"Raises are definitely fun."

"I notice you have several high-interest credit cards, some as high as 22%. That's a lot of dough going down the drain unnecessarily. Have you looked into different credit cards to help you consolidate, ones that offer 0% interest on balance transfers?"

"We've done some credit card consolidation in the past, but that was right before the economy took its nosedive," I told him. "All the cards we've seen since then have offered higher interest rates—but maybe we weren't looking hard enough. And we were turned down from the cards we did apply for because of the credit card debt we had already racked up."

"I'm not a credit expert, but I've found that using 0% interest credit cards can make a big difference. You'll typically pay a balance transfer fee of 3%, but it's usually well worth it, depending on how big the balance is. Your Firestone card with only $600 on it—I wouldn't worry about transferring that one. But if you could take a couple of these that you're paying 20% on and put them on a 0% card, and that would free up some cash that you could put toward paying down the first debt on your chart, which is the larger Firestone card.

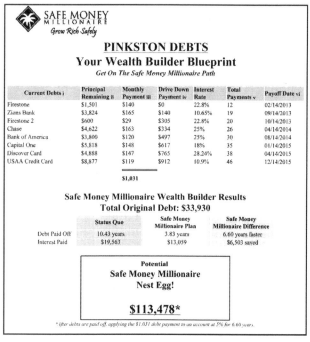

SAFE MONEY MILLIONAIRE
Grow Rich Safely

PINKSTON DEBTS
Your Wealth Builder Blueprint
Get On The Safe Money Millionaire Path

Current Debts i	Principal Remaining ii	Monthly Payment iii	Drive Down Payment iv	Interest Rate	Total Payments v	Payoff Date vi
Firestone	$1,501	$140	$0	22.8%	12	02/14/2013
Zions Bank	$3,824	$165	$140	10.65%	19	09/14/2013
Firestone 2	$600	$29	$305	22.8%	20	10/14/2013
Chase	$4,622	$163	$334	25%	26	04/14/2014
Bank of America	$3,800	$120	$497	25%	30	08/14/2014
Capital One	$5,818	$148	$617	18%	35	01/14/2015
Discover Card	$4,888	$147	$765	28.24%	38	04/14/2015
USAA Credit Card	$8,877	$119	$912	10.9%	46	12/14/2015
	$1,031					

Safe Money Millionaire Wealth Builder Results
Total Original Debt: $33,930

	Status Quo	Safe Money Millionaire Plan	Safe Money Millionaire Difference
Debt Paid Off	10.43 years	3.83 years	6.60 years faster
Interest Paid	$19,563	$13,059	$6,503 saved

**Potential
Safe Money Millionaire
Nest Egg!**

$113,478*

* After debts are paid off, applying the $1,031 debt payment to an account at 5% for 6.60 years.

"Another way to find money is to do your own debt consolidation. Do you have a car loan?"

"We just have the van payment," I explained. "That's the Zions Bank loan. We have a smaller car that's already paid off."

"I'm going to throw some ideas at you, and you can take them or leave them. One would be to get a larger loan on one of the cars you currently have. I'm pulling up the Blue Book on what your van might be worth. They're saying it's worth around $4500. You have a loan for $3800. It might not be worth doing a refinance and getting some cash out, but we can look. If you financed it for $4500 or even a little more—sometimes banks will lend a little more than Blue Book—and got enough money back to pay off your smaller Firestone bill, you've just freed up $30. Your monthly payment on the van would go up a little, but not that much. That's one of the ways to find money that most people don't think about.

"What about your other car? You could see what a bank would lend you on it. If you borrowed $1500 on it and paid off the larger Firestone bill, sure, you'd have a car payment again, but it would only be around $34. Right now, you're paying $140 a month to Firestone. You use the car loan funds to pay them off, take on a $34 car payment, and now you've created $104 a month, which you would then use to pay off your other bills. So right there we've already freed up $134 and saved money on interest, because your Firestone bills do have very high interest rates."

"I never would have thought of that," I said. "In my mind, because the second car was paid off, it was paid *off*, and it wasn't on my radar anymore."

"There is a sense of satisfaction that comes from having a car paid off," Brett replied. "But it's certainly an option to leverage it this way. Now, in your situation you might not be eligible for some of the credit cards out there, but I'm surprised at the lines of credit they are still dishing out. What I would recommend is applying to several credit card companies at the same time. If you apply for multiple lines of credit within a seven-to-fourteen day window, they will show up on your credit score as one hit."

"I didn't know that," I said. "I thought every single inquiry showed up as a separate hit."

"They've set it up to show as one hit because of the way people shop around," Brett explained. "If someone is purchasing a car or a home, they'll talk to several different lending groups before settling on one, and it's not fair for their credit score to suffer for it when it's all done for the same purchase. So if you're going to apply for credit, do it all at the same time so the companies don't look at your report and say you've had too many inquiries."

"Quick question," I said. "What do you think about talking to a bank about a debt consolidation loan?"

"I would definitely look into that. As we've discussed, many of the debt consolidation companies out there are unscrupulous, but a bank is entirely different. With your situation, a couple of small moves could really help you free up some cash and help speed the process of getting out of debt. So talk to the bank, see about a loan, and talk about refinancing your vehicles. Do you know what your credit scores are?"

"They're not great, but they're not terrible." I gave him the exact totals.

"Yeah, not off the charts, but doable. I would definitely talk to the bank. Okay, let's look at your other debts here for a minute. Tell me about your USAA credit card."

"We used that a few years ago to do some debt consolidation, but when the money was freed up, it got sucked up into other expenses, and we didn't roll it over into our other debts. We just ended up with more debt."

"This is why it's so important to have a debt plan and a spending plan. If you don't have those in place when you consolidate, the issues that got you into debt in the first place haven't been resolved, and you're just setting yourself up. Don't prepare to consolidate until you're sure you're not going to get yourself in trouble again.

"With the Drive Down debt report in front of you, it will help you to avoid this, but ultimately it comes back to taking the ten seconds to write down your expenses when you buy something.

"I've mentioned using a Smartphone app. Just seeing how much money is being wasted on interest and developing a hatred for debt has really been a motivating force in my life. I actually had a sheet on my pantry door that had all my debts written on it, and one by one I crossed them out. I loved it. It became my mission to annihilate my debt as quickly as possible. And it's amazing that when you focus on something, it happens.

"Cultivate an attitude in your family that you abhor debt—you don't want anything to do with it. Then when you increase your income, it will go toward paying down the debt instead of flying out the door.

"This will take discipline and hard work, no doubt about it," Brett said. "No one wants to live on beans and rice forever. But the truth is, you don't have to. You can eat out. You can go on wonderful vacations, buy a nice home, drive a nice car, and go shopping at the mall. You can have anything you want. In fact, you need a release once in a while or else life just gets too monotonous—and the whole process breaks down.

"People get into trouble when they allow their emotions to control their buying decisions. They impulse buy. They put things on credit because they want it now or 'they deserve it.' The simple solution to all of this is simple: Just plan to spend!"

"You want me to plan to spend?" I asked. "Sounds a little counterintuitive to me."

"That's right. Give yourself permission right now to spend money on the things you want every month. Do you want a nice cruise with your spouse for next year's anniversary?"

"Well, sure. Who doesn't? But come on—how am I going to pull that one off?"

"Easy. Just calculate the cost and start allocating money for it right now. Don't wait until it's here, and then put it on a credit card. I said you can have anything you want. You just can't have everything you want. So if you want a nice vacation, that might mean no shopping for clothes at the mall for a couple of months. Is it worth the trade-off? It's up to you . . . it's your money, your choice."

"Okay, that makes a little more sense to me."

"This is what we call 'having a spending plan.' No one wants to live under the negativity of a budget. The truth is, budgets don't work very well because they are based on a guilt-driven concept of what you can't have. However, everyone knows they need to keep their spending under control.

"So here's the deal. Your spending plan will have your monthly expenses on it. It will have the 10% (hopefully) you are paying yourself into your wealth account for savings, and then it has your 'eating out' money, 'big trip' money, or what I call, your 'fun money.' Plan for a certain amount of fun money every month. Just put it into your spending plan. Open a new account at the bank, if you need to keep it separated. Or put more into a 101 Plan™ so it can earn interest while you aren't using it—we'll talk about the 101 Plan™ in a minute. Once you've decided you each have $50 or $150 or $300—whatever amount of fun money you choose—spend it every month and don't feel guilty about it!

"Be sure to keep track of it by writing it down. When you do that, I promise you'll enjoy life in a whole new way because you aren't stressed and feeling guilty about every little thing you buy."

"That sounds really good," I replied. "I like the idea of planning to spend, and then of course, doing the spending. Now, I have another question. I want to have some money in savings so we don't have to rely on credit when things go wrong. We've done that a lot, and it's really difficult. We've always tried to live frugally, but there's never been anything left over, so when we get hit with something like car repairs, those go on the credit card, and so we've just increased our debt load. If our goal is to get out of debt, we can't keep adding to our existing debt load."

"I've been there. Trust me, I've been there," Brett said. "When I started out, I was paid strictly on commission—in fact, I've worked that way my whole life! Our first Christmas as a married couple, our grand total of income was $347, so we ate Pizza Pockets from 7-Eleven for Christmas dinner. At other times, I'd have more income, and I'd use it to pay off the debt we had accumulated when things were tight. For a lot of years, that's how we lived. It was a crazy cycle, so I know what it's like.

"Now, if you guys got creative, you might be able to pay off the smaller Firestone bill with one of your lower interest rate credit cards, and you could pay off the larger Firestone bill by refinancing your cars, and that would create $170 a month that you're no longer paying Firestone, and you're no longer paying the high interest rate. Talk to Matt and see what he thinks, and talk to the bank as well. And talk to the credit card companies—you might not get 0%, but you might get 3%. As long as you know you're not going to turn around and spend that money on something else, but keep putting it toward your debt, that would be a really positive move.

"You brought me a list of your monthly expenses, right?"

I pulled a sheet of paper from my purse and handed it to him, and he looked it over.

"I see on here that you have a storage unit."

"Yes, we do. Because we live in a trailer home, we don't have much storage space, so we rent a unit. It's $49 a month, but we used to have a larger unit that was $75. We went through it and got rid of everything except what we really wanted to keep, and saved ourselves $26 a month that way."

"Do you have a relative with extra space who would let you store your things at their house instead?"

"No, I'm afraid not," I replied. "Although, if I did, that would be a great way to save some money."

"Okay, let's look at your Internet and phone. How often have you looked at alternatives?"

"We haven't for a little while."

"You might look into that. There's a company called magicJack that allows you to pay $20 for unlimited phone calling for a year."

"Seriously?"

"Yes. Right now, you're spending about $26 per month on your phone, and magicJack would cut that down to basically zero. Now we've freed up $195.

"Moving on down your list here—I'm glad to see that you have life insurance. This is critical to a sound financial plan. *Everyone* should have at least a minimum amount if they have a spouse or kids. It's just negligence if a parent doesn't do this. You're paying $56 a month for coverage for your whole family, so you might not get a much better deal. But I imagine you could save something. I can refer you to someone to help you with that. In 2008, the life insurance rates came down, so you might get more coverage for less money."

"That would be great."

"And talk to me about car insurance."

"We have two cars with two drivers, and I believe we have full coverage. I'll have to check with my husband for sure on that."

"I would recommend looking into other car insurance companies as well. When was the last time you shopped around?"

"We never really have," I replied. "My husband had this policy when we got married, and we just added on to it as needed."

"I would definitely look around. How is your driving record?"

"Pretty near perfect."

"I suggest that you check with a local independent agent who represents multiple carriers. I would expect that you could pay around $40 or $50 a month for your two cars. That's one of the first places people save money—shopping their car insurance.

"Now, here's the big opportunity. How much is your tax refund each year?"

"It varies, but we usually get between two thousand and three thousand a year."

"And how much interest does the IRS pay you for letting them borrow your money?"

I blinked. "Um . . . nothing. They just take it."

"Exactly. Every year, the IRS takes money out of your paycheck and withholds it from you, and then they give some of it back. You're essentially giving them a loan, and you aren't getting anything out of it for yourself."

"So . . . what do I do about it?" Brett had pretty much lost me on this one. I had no idea at all how to fight the IRS.

"Look at your withholdings. You don't have to let the IRS take so much out of your paycheck—you can determine how much is taken out per month."

Oh, now I understood. "So instead of getting $2000 in refunds once a year, they'd be taking a little less out of my check per month—like, getting my refund a little at a time all year long."

"Exactly. An average tax refund in this country equates to $281 per month or $3372 per year, so imagine receiving that amount every month. Would that help your financial situation?"

"Absolutely."

Brett looked over my sheet. "Are you writing off your Internet, cell phone, and mileage? You have a home-based business—you should be deducting everything you use for that business."

I suddenly felt a little sheepish. "I haven't been writing off my Internet, which is my chief business tool. We're turning in our taxes this week—I'll make sure we get it on there."

"Good. People who have home-based businesses need to pay attention to every expense. Office supplies, computers, printers, postage—if you spend money on it for your business, it should be on your spreadsheet."

Brett slid my paper back across the table to me. "Now, you've given me an itemized list of your expenses, but what I would like for you to do now, either this month or next, is to pay close attention to everything you spend on a day-to-day basis. Five dollars here, ten dollars there, whatever the case may be. Track your spending and see if it truly comes up to these numbers. Then you'll know if you're actually spending what you think you are, and you'll be able to control it.

"Based on this list, there aren't a lot of places where you can save money. You can probably save a little on car insurance and on your phone and Internet, and doing those two things might bring you $45-$50 you can put toward your Drive Down payments on your debts. Focus on consolidating your debts and refinancing. If you were able to get new car loans and to use your credit cards to pay off your other debts, you'd free up $195 a month. Add to it the $200 per month in taxes, and we've just given you a raise of almost $400 per month!"

"Wow, I can't believe it," I said. "I thought you were going to have a really hard time saving us anything."

"Actually, so did I. After looking at your limited expenses, I didn't know how much we'd be able to accomplish, but by doing just a few of these things, you'll be able to put an extra $400 to driving down your debt, and let me show you what that does:

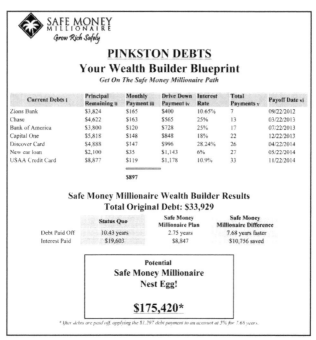

"How does it make you feel knowing that you can literally be out of debt in less than three years, you'll have saved over $10,000 in interest, and be able to build a nest egg of $175,000 during the exact same time you would have been just paying off your original debt?"

"I'm completely floored," I said. I studied the figures on the new Wealth Builder Blueprint. "Really, I'm floored. And it takes a lot to floor me."

Brett laughed. "Great. We're also going to talk about how to amplify your income. You and your husband both work from home, in addition to your husband's job, and there are so many ways you can maximize your reach and alternative ways you can make money. My sister probably makes about $500 a month getting things for free off classified sites like Craigslist and then turning around and selling them. There are several things you can do that are as simple as that. We've laid out several proven models to increase your income by $500 to $5000 per month in the Income Amplifier program, and you can take a look at them and see what works for you. If you're able to find a way to get some larger chunks of money and wipe out these debts, it's fun. It's exciting to see this stuff disappear. We can only save so much—and in your case specifically there's not a lot we can do to crunch down your expenses. But we can get more money coming to you."

"I think the key to this whole thing—and you talk about this in *Safe Money Millionaire*—is that people are used to living the status quo," I said. "We just all think, well, this is how it is. In talking to you and talking to Ethan, my eyes have been opened a lot. We've had our noses to the grindstone for so long that looking up and around and seeing what else is out there is mind-boggling. I'm excited to look into this process and take control of it."

> Visit
> www.milliondollardiva.com
> to see how the
> **Income Amplifier**
> can increase your income
> by $500 to $5000 per month
> . . . in your spare time.

"I'm glad, because this is what I live for," Brett replied. "I love helping people have these kinds of realizations. And I can't wait to help you get into a situation where you're out of debt and living a happier life."

"I really appreciate it," I told him. "Now, for my homework, you'd like me to write down everything I spend and compare it to my estimates so I'm sure I really am spending what I think I'm spending. Then I'm going to go over the Income Amplifier with my husband. We're going to look into different car insurance and phone options. We'll also look at different credit card options and see if we can consolidate. And we'll talk to our bank. We'll also check our withholdings on our taxes and get them lowered."

"Exactly. See how much of that you're able to accomplish, and each month you can chart your progress by using the Drive Down debt software.

"But this is just the beginning. Paying off your debts doesn't make you a Million Dollar Diva—the next thing I'll show you is how to actually become wealthy. While you're working on your debts, you can also be growing your wealth, and what I'm about to show you will blow your mind."

See Tristi's Plan In Action!

See her successes and challenges, and follow her monthly progress of driving down her debt and building her million-dollar retirement by visiting:

www.milliondollardiva.com

Chapter 8

Million Dollar Diva
on Autopilot

"Now, I promised I'd blow your mind," Brett said. "I promise not to let you down. Let me ask—where is your current financial path taking you? Where are you going to be in ten or twenty years, or at retirement age, if you continue doing what you're doing?"

"Well, after looking at our debts, it looked like in ten years we'd still be paying them off. In twenty years, I have no clue. And for retirement . . . it looks bleak. Very bleak." I laughed. "Yeah, I'd say we're pretty much moving in with our kids when we retire. Hope they have room for us."

"What would you say if I told you that without earning a dime more than you make right now, you could be a millionaire when you retire?"

"I would say, come again? How could our small income produce a million dollars?"

"I understand your skepticism, but you have me and Ethan on your side. Let me show you how it's possible. We found an additional $400 we could use to pay off your debt, right?"

"Right."

"And based on everything you've learned so far in this process, do you believe I know what I'm talking about and I'm not going to lead you astray?"

"You've given me hope and opened my eyes at every turn, and you've been remarkably generous with your time," I said. "Yes, I trust that you're giving me the real deal."

"Good, because I am. Now I'm going to suggest that instead of putting all $400 toward paying down your debt, you take half of it and start your wealth account. No matter what situation you're in, you absolutely, positively must start today to pay yourself. That's one of the keys to making this process work. Start to create momentum now— start the plan today so that once you've paid off your debts, it's easy for you to keep the plan going.

"Becoming a Million Dollar Diva requires both sides of the coin—paying off your debts, and starting your wealth account. And I mean today. Not tomorrow. Not next year. Not after your debts are paid off. It's time for you to start treating yourself with some self-respect. The question you have to answer is this: Are you worth the investment? Are your family, your marriage, and your dream worth it?"

"Absolutely. Everything I do is for our family, for our kids."

"Then it's time to start treating them like they're the top priority financially. That means paying yourself *first*. Not last, not never . . . not paying all the bills, the credit cards, the bankers, the interest, the retailers, and then having nothing left to show for it. *The Richest Man in Babylon* is a book many consider to be the most powerful in history for growing wealth, and the very first principle taught is to pay yourself first.

"Have I made myself clear?"

"Crystal," I said.

"Okay, now I know it doesn't make 'math sense' to be putting money into an account that might be earning less interest than you could pay off by applying it to your debts, but we already know money isn't about math—"

"It's about emotions. I know, I know," I said with a smile.

"Okay, so here's the deal. I want you to take half the money and use it to pay down your debts using the Drive Down report we've created together. I've revised it to show $200 instead of $400. The interesting thing is that it doesn't take much longer to pay it off than it would if you were paying $400, because of the power of the Drive Down momentum. With $400, it would take two years and nine months, and with $200, it only takes about nine months longer. During that time, you've built up a nice little wealth account. You're already on your way.

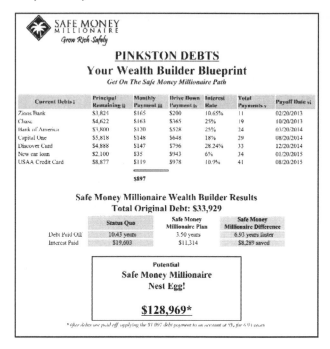

SAFE MONEY MILLIONAIRE
MILLIONAIRE
Grow Rich Safely

PINKSTON DEBTS
Your Wealth Builder Blueprint
Get On The Safe Money Millionaire Path

Current Debts i	Principal Remaining ii	Monthly Payment iii	Drive Down Payment iv	Interest Rate	Total Payments v	Payoff Date vi
Zions Bank	$3,824	$165	$200	10.65%	11	02/20/2013
Chase	$4,622	$163	$365	25%	19	10/20/2013
Bank of America	$3,800	$120	$528	25%	24	03/20/2014
Capital One	$5,818	$148	$648	18%	29	08/20/2014
Discover Card	$4,888	$147	$796	28.24%	33	12/20/2014
New car loan	$2,100	$35	$943	6%	34	01/20/2015
USAA Credit Card	$8,877	$119	$978	10.9%	41	08/20/2015

$897

Safe Money Millionaire Wealth Builder Results
Total Original Debt: $33,929

	Status Quo	Safe Money Millionaire Plan	Safe Money Millionaire Difference
Debt Paid Off	10.43 years	3.50 years	6.93 years faster
Interest Paid	$19,603	$11,314	$8,289 saved

Potential
Safe Money Millionaire
Nest Egg!

$128,969*

After debts are paid off applying the $1,097 debt payment to an account at 5%, for 6.93 years

"This is also important for people who have mortgages, because even by using the Drive Down plan, they will often be paying a mortgage for over ten years. That's a ton of time lost if you aren't growing and compounding your wealth along the way. Make sense?"

"Definitely. It's pretty sad if they could have been saving money the whole time, and weren't doing it."

"Most people run out of steam before they get to this point—that's why you've got to start now.

But here's where it gets exciting. What's going to happen after your last debt is paid off in three and a half years?"

"I'm going to throw a big party, and possibly name a child after you," I said. "That would be awkward if it was a girl, though. Brettina, maybe?"

"Um, yeah, in addition to that, now that all your debts are paid off, where are you going to put the $1097 that was going to pay down your debt?"

"Into my wealth account?"

"Exactly. You can now use it to grow your *own* wealth instead of the bankers' and lenders'. Now check this out—if you use one of the Safe Money Millionaire financial strategies I'm going to share with you, and take the $200 you're already paying every month, and then add the $1097 to it, you could have approximately 1.1 million dollars waiting for you at age 65, and have $107,000 in annual retirement income from age 65 to age 100. That's $107,000 passive cash flow every year to do whatever you want with until age 100.

"Along the way you can use your money to go on vacations, send kids to college, even buy a house if you want—and then pay your wealth account back instead of a bank or credit card. You can even pay yourself extra interest to grow your wealth faster. It's never at risk like it might be in the market, so you don't have to worry about market crashes. And it grows tax-deferred, and you access it tax-free, so it's really like having an extra

20-30% because it's not getting hammered by taxes when you want to use it."

"And what's it called?"

"I call it Millionaire Autopilot because it doesn't take any study or work or effort on your part. It works extremely well. But there are a couple of different financial strategies that can help you get wealthy safely. Let me show you what they are."

Chapter 9

INVESTING TO GROW RICH SAFELY

As you—hopefully—noticed, the subtitle of this book is "The Smart Woman's Guide to Getting Rich Safely." I like the "Getting Rich Safely" part—emphasis on "Safely." I've heard of people losing their shirts in the stock market or in their 401(k) plan, and that worries me. I'm not a risk taker. I would rather know what I have, and live on what I have, than to place my money somewhere completely out of my control.

But I also know that you can place your money wisely and create a better foundation for your future.

I recall seeing my grandmother live on a very tight budget in her later years. Children don't often think about how their grandparents live, but as I got older, I noticed how carefully she had to watch every penny. In watching her, it occurred to me that after retirement, money can become very tight. With all these issues in mind, I decided I would ask Brett some questions about investing, retirement, and where my husband and I can put our money to grow it safely.

Brett smiled. "I can't tell you how many times I've heard that question. It's a very good question, too, because if you do it wrong, you could lose big time—like millions of people have in recent years. I had to learn the hard way myself. After losing a significant amount of money in a market crash, Ethan and I went on a quest to discover investment alternatives that help people get rich *safely*. We call them Safe Money Millionaire strategies, and we'll share a few of them with you in just a second.

"Now, you've seen *Alice in Wonderland*, right? Do you remember the scene where Alice asks the Cheshire Cat if he can help her find her way? The cat says that her path will depend on where she wants to go. If she doesn't have a destination in mind, it doesn't matter what path she takes.

"We already know where you want to go. We've spoken about your dreams of getting out of debt, having the freedom and time to write as much as you want, whenever you want, being able to own a nice home, travel with your family, write that book in Paris, and ultimately be able to retire with an income that will allow you to live without worry about money."

"I also want a huge library in my house," I said. "With overstuffed chairs, mahogany shelves with books top to bottom . . . the works. Maybe a mini fridge I could put right next to my reading couch . . . I don't remember if I mentioned that or not."

"That's great—the bigger, the better. Now that you have your dreams clearly outlined and you know what you want, it matters—a lot—which way we go from here. Not all paths will lead to that destination."

Brett settled back in his chair. "Most people are looking for the same things financially—although they might not all want a huge library or an Air Nautique ski boat. They're saving for a rainy day, they want to get out of debt, they would like to travel to some fun and exotic places, and they ultimately hope to quit working someday, financially secure. This means having enough passive income from your savings or investments to cover your monthly expenses, whether you work or not. Financial security isn't about being so rich you fly on private jets—it's simply knowing you'll always have what you need. How would life be right now if you had enough income from your investments to cover expenses every month?"

I took a second to imagine that scenario. "I could go for that . . . yes, I could totally go for that. I would love to take days or even weeks off from work and still be able to pay my bills. That's certainly not how things are right now."

"It's a lot easier to get there than most people think, and I'm going to show you how to make it happen. But it's impossible to make progress if you don't beat the enemies of wealth, so I have to warn you . . . I don't do 'stupid.' I don't want you to just know enough to be dangerous—it's important that you be fully informed, more educated than ninety percent of the people in this country who blindly follow the sheep in front of them right off the cliff. Are you okay with that?"

I grinned. "I don't do stupid, either. Yes, please— tell me what I need to know."

"Great. So let's talk about the tools and products you can use to get what you want financially. And remember, we're looking for income and ways to grow your money safely while beating the enemies of wealth. Do you know what those are?"

"I'm probably well acquainted with them, although I'm not sure I could name them all."

"I'll make it easy on you—there are four of them," Brett said. "The first is the loss of your money, meaning that your investments or your 401(k) actually shrink instead of grow. Then there are taxes, interest, and inflation. Each of these can kill your wealth, if you let them. They're like banditos hiding along the road to financial security who trick you into stopping to help, and then they steal your car and leave you on the side of the road. You never can be too careful.

"Now I'll give you a quick rundown on each of the enemies, and then I'll answer your question about what product you should use to beat them.

The first enemy is market loss. I'm sure you've heard the old parable of the wise man and the foolish man."

"Of course! And I'm guessing you probably don't want me to burst into song right now."

"Maybe later," Brett said. "It reads like this: 'The wise man built his house upon a rock: And the rain descended, and the floods came, and the winds blew, and beat upon that house; and it fell not: for it was founded upon a rock. And the foolish man built his house upon the sand: And the rain descended, and the floods came, and the winds blew, and beat upon that house; and it fell: and great was the fall of it.'

"This is the first rule of being a Safe Money Millionaire, and of course it also translates into being a Million Dollar Diva. You *never, ever, ever* want to lose your money. Loss of principle is devastating to your wealth. Once you lose money, it can take substantially longer to make it back up—and you've lost out on that time forever.

"For example, if your money in a mutual fund or 401(k) goes down 40%, you actually have to get a 65% return to get back to even."

"65%? Is that even possible?"

"If the market average is 8% per year, you'd be looking at eight years just to get back what you lost! It's like someone robbed you of eight years of your financial life."

"That sounds pretty devastating," I said. "I don't know too many people who would be able to keep their spirits up for eight years waiting for things to settle back down."

Brett nodded. "Agreed. Now, this next point is worth writing down. Warren Buffet's two rules of investing are:

> #1. Never lose the principle.
> #2. Never forget rule #1.

"That makes sense to me, but how do you keep from losing it? Isn't it just something that happens as the market fluctuates? I didn't know a person could really help it."

"That's a good question," Brett said. "Think about 401(k)s, mutual funds, and other stock investments. They don't follow rule number one, so what does that tell you?"

"They aren't the vehicle to get me to my destination." I was starting to wonder what the right vehicle would be—Brett had just discounted everything I'd been considering.

"401(k)s and IRAs can be traps for multiple reasons. They often expose your retirement savings to complete risk. But that's just the tip of the iceberg. Contrary to popular belief, often the investments in your 401(k)s are not 'savings' at all. The definition of 'savings' is the root of the word: *safe*. Everyone needs a foundation of 'safe money' that's there for them in case of a rainy day, and especially for retirement income. Savings should be your safety net.

"Once you have a foundation of income you can count on for retirement, you can take a greater risk with your extra money, if you want. Investing is defined by risk. It can bring greater returns. But you can also lose your money. That's fine if you have money you can afford to lose. But many people simply don't ever get there . . . and most find out that losing their money is a sickening roller coaster ride that they'd rather not experience again."

I leaned forward a little bit. "I'd love to have enough money to create options, but I'm not a risk taker, like I mentioned to you before—the idea of losing money doesn't sit well with me. But we need to grow the money somehow, right? I don't imagine you'd counsel me to leave it in the bank where it's getting practically no interest."

"We do need to grow your money because of the second enemy of wealth—inflation. Leaving your money in the bank or in a mattress can be almost as risky as investing in the stock market—especially depending on the inflation rate. You're familiar with the concept of inflation?"

"Mostly as it relates to the rising cost of goods," I said. "I know there are other ways it comes into play, but basically, it means that your money is losing value, right?"

"Right. Inflation is essentially sucking the worth of your dollars away from you. Five years ago, fifty cents could buy a soda, but now it takes a dollar. That's the way we see inflation in our daily lives— it takes more money to buy the same thing today as it did in the past.

"The Federal Reserve and the government essentially determine the inflation rate by how much money they print and put into circulation. It's about supply and demand. When there are too many dollars in circulation, the worth goes down.

"In fact, the dollar has lost 70% of its value since 1970 because the government has been printing money like crazy. Here's something you won't hear from the gurus on TV or in *Money Magazine*: the government's 'official' inflation rate is fake."

"I knew it! Oh, sorry . . . please, go on."

"Basically, the yardstick for inflation was changed because it's easier for the government to feed the people a lower inflation rate than a high one. Inflation at the reported rate of 4% sounds a heck of a lot better than 10%, doesn't it? It's an easy way for the government to hide how inept and corrupt it has become."

"So if I've done my mental math right, that means I need to grow my money by 8-10% just to stay even?"

"For now, yes, that's probably about right."

Score a point for my mental math. "Well, how do I do that?"

"I'll show you some options here in a minute, but first we have two more enemies to beat—taxes and interest. I call interest the 'vampire'—and not in the 'Twilight' sort of way . . ."

"So, no sparklies in the sunshine?"

"Nope, sorry. These are the *bad* vampires, the ones who stick their fangs into your neck and suck the financial life out of you, leaving you like a zombie . . . still moving, but not really alive. Sound familiar?"

"I can relate to being a part of the living dead financially. No matter what we do, it seems like everyone gets paid but us. By the time we're done paying all our bills—with those high interest rates— there's nothing left over." I motioned to the debt analysis sheet on the table between us.

"It's a terrible way to live, yet most people are in that exact situation. According to Nelson Nash, the average American is paying up to 34.5% of their after-tax income straight to interest . . . not even including principle."

"Wow. At least we're not alone." I guess misery really does love company, huh?

Brett pulled out his wallet. "Imagine taking a twenty-dollar bill and ripping a third of it off for taxes and another third for interest. What's left is yours to pay the bills, live on, and build your savings."

I shook my head. "And then we wonder why we feel like we're living paycheck to paycheck . . . we only get to use one third of our money."

"Exactly." Brett returned his wallet to his pocket. "In a minute, I'll show you how to defeat the interest vampire. We'll talk about paying yourself interest instead of paying your bankers and credit card companies.

"Now let's talk about the last enemy: the tax man. This one is really tricky because of all the different ways the tax man gets his hands in your pocketbook. Thomas Jefferson said, 'An income tax of 1% is equivalent to slavery.'"

"That's a great quote—I love Thomas Jefferson." I thought for a second. "But we do need some taxes, don't we?"

"Sure, some taxes are necessary to maintain roads, infrastructure, and protect our nation. But most people don't realize all the taxes they are paying. Just take a look at this list for a second." Brett pushed a piece of paper across the table to me.

It read:

- Accounts Receivable Tax
- Building Permit Tax
- Capital Gains Tax

- CDL License Tax
- Cigarette Tax
- Corporate Income Tax
- Court Fines (indirect taxes)
- Dog License Tax
- Federal Income Tax
- Federal Unemployment Tax (FUTA)
- Fishing License Tax
- Food License Tax
- Fuel Permit Tax
- Gasoline Tax (42¢ per gallon)
- Hunting License Tax
- Inheritance Tax Interest Expense (tax on the money)
- Inventory Tax IRS Interest Charges (tax on top of tax)
- IRS Penalties (tax on top of tax)
- Liquor Tax
- Local Income Tax
- Luxury Taxes
- Marriage License Tax
- Medicare Tax
- Property Tax
- Real Estate Tax
- Sales Tax
- School Tax
- Septic Permit Tax
- Service Charge Tax
- Social Security Tax
- State Income Tax
- State Unemployment Tax
- Recreational Vehicle Tax
- Road Toll Booth Tax

- Road Usage Taxes (Truckers)
- Telephone (federal excise tax)
- Telephone (federal universal service fee tax)
- Telephone (federal, state, and local surcharge taxes)
- Telephone (minimum usage surcharge tax)
- Telephone (recurring and non-recurring charges tax)
- Telephone (state and local tax)
- Telephone (usage charge tax)
- Toll Bridge Tax
- Toll Tunnel Tax
- Traffic Fines (indirect taxation)
- Trailer Registration Tax
- Utility Tax
- Vehicle License Registration Tax
- Vehicle Sales Tax
- Watercraft Registration Tax
- Well Permit Tax
- Workers Compensation Tax

"Wow," I said, skimming down the list. "This is insane! But what can we do about it?"

"Remember the Boston Tea Party?"

I grinned. "Are you saying we should dress up in costumes? Probably not, huh . . . sorry. I just do enjoy costumes. Yes, the colonists were upset at the taxes being levied by the British. They didn't have any say as to what was happening to them. One of their rallying cries was 'No taxation without representation'—they wanted their voices to be heard."

"You got it. Unfortunately, now we have taxation *despite* representation. Often, it's our own citizens who load the gun, point it at their own foot, and pull the trigger . . . we shoot ourselves by constantly voting to increase our own taxes."

"What do you mean?" Who would vote to increase their taxes? That would just be silly.

"Have you ever seen a proposal on the ballot that sounds like a good idea, like maintaining the local zoo? Those things take bonds, and those bonds are put on the ballot. This is usually nothing more than us voting for a new tax to be paid. They are great at spinning it to sound really small, like 'It's equivalent to just a few pennies per day per tax payer.'"

"Ah, yes, bonds. That does sound familiar. Yeah, it doesn't sound like much when they put it that way . . . the whole 'spin' thing."

"Exactly, and who wants to be the bad guy, voting against keeping the zoo animals cozy in their new facility?"

"Not me. I love animals."

"Of course—everyone does, and that's why many people just mark the box 'Yes.' Like the frog in the pot of water, we keep turning up the heat until we eventually boil ourselves to death."

"So you vote against all bonds that appear on the ballot?"

"Always. I never vote for a bond, or a tax increase, *no matter what*. Why would I voluntarily give even more of my money to politicians who spend like drunken sailors? No thanks. "

I nodded. "But what if it really is a good cause? We have to maintain our cities and roads, things like that."

"The government will *always* find a way to finance what's most important. But they never try to cut costs, be more efficient, or be more effective with our money if they know they can just go to the public for a blank check whenever they want. I'd much rather see them get creative and be forced to cut costs rather than asking for more money. Look at the situation it's gotten us into with the federal government deficit—they never cut costs. They just go get more money. It's a broken system, and it needs to be fixed.

"So let me get off my soap box of death by a thousand paper cuts of fees and taxes. Let's get to the big tax time bomb most people have ticking right under their seat and don't even know it . . . their retirement.

"So many people are guided to qualified 'tax-deferred' programs with horribly misleading information about savings in taxes. The truth is, you may be saving taxes today by putting them off until tomorrow, but once the time comes to access your money in retirement, it's a very rude awakening. You may save a few dollars today, but if you crunch the numbers, you could end up paying five times more in taxes than what you saved."

"You're right—I bet most people are completely unaware of that." I was, until he explained it.

"401(k)s and IRAs have been sold as gospel truth to the American public on the basis of what's best for Wall Street's profits, not what's best for the consumer. These plans make bankers and stock brokers *billions*, with trillions of dollars being held in them . . . and they get a percentage of the amount invested."

"So they get paid based on the amount of money their clients invest . . . not on performance. Right?"

"Yup," Brett said. "They don't really care if your money grows or not because they get paid either way. Another frustration people have with qualified plans is all the strings attached with accessing your money. It's your money, you earned it, but you can't use it!"

"It's stupid that you can't access your own money. It sounds like this is all rigged for Wall Street's benefit."

"What if you have an emergency surgery, "Brett asked, "a big unexpected expense, or want to buy a new house? It's your money . . . but not really. I've always hated that about qualified plans. A good financial foundation will always have liquidity, or access to your money when you need it. To me, a qualified plan is like having life jackets locked away behind bulletproof glass, and when the boat crashes, you can see the life jackets while you're drowning. They're right there—you just can't use them to save yourself."

"Sounds like a bizarre form of torture." It also sounded like a great scene in a book. I'd have to file that away for later. "And I always thought 401(k)s were the way to do it because they're so popular. What should my husband and I be doing instead? In addition to avoiding all boat rides in the future, because I'm kind of creeped out right now . . ."

Brett smiled. "There are some options I really like for an incredibly effective portfolio. You may not have heard of most of them. Before we head into that, here are some Million Dollar Diva rules for you to remember before considering any investment:

- Always have access to your money
- Never lose money in stock market crashes
- Grow your money with as many tax advantages as possible
- Have assets that spin off passive income
- Hedge against inflation
- Defeat the interest vampire

"Now with that said, let's start with silver coins."

This surprised me. "Silver? I thought gold was all the rage."

"Silver's not the most popular investment, but it's powerful for a couple of important reasons. First, you can start small. You can buy silver for thirty to fifty bucks for a one-ounce coin."

"And I imagine that fluctuates."

"Yes, and that is one of the negatives of silver investing. It's not going to spin off passive income, and it's at the mercy of what the market says it's worth. But it's never worth zero. That's a major benefit—when inflation is going up the way it is now, silver always performs better. Investing in precious metals can help you hedge against inflation.

"In addition, it's liquid—meaning you can almost always use it to purchase something or get US dollars for it immediately, if needed. So it's great to have in emergencies."

"So tell me why you prefer silver to gold. Or do you suggest purchasing gold as well?"

"It's really very simple. I prefer silver because it's a heck of a lot cheaper than gold. Today you can buy an ounce of gold for $1750, or you can buy an ounce of silver for $32. For most people, silver is just more practical as they're getting started.

"On the downside, silver is more volatile than gold, so the price moves around a bit more. We're not going to depend on silver for our entire retirement. However, it is a great place to get started, and you get to *buy* something. It's like killing two birds with one stone. You get the emotional charge of buying something cool, and you get the monetary reward of having increased your savings. You can't beat that!"

"I like that idea. How much money would you recommend I put into gold and silver? Once I have money to invest, of course."

"That's always helpful. I would recommend silver and gold as a 'safety net,' not a retirement plan. It doesn't create passive income, which is what you need in retirement. So depending on how much you have to save each month, I'd suggest putting up to 10% of the total amount you are saving into silver. Of course, if the price goes up dramatically, you can sell it for a profit, but that's not my recommended strategy. Just buy it and hold it for emergency use and to help hedge against inflation.

"Now let's talk about market-linked CDs. Most people have heard of CDs and have a level of comfort with them. Do you know what a CD is?"

"I know you're not talking about music, but I have to confess, I don't know what it stands for."

"It's a Certificate of Deposit. It's a financial product you can put your money into, and has two things going for it: it's secure—it's FDIC insured, just like a bank account, and it gives you a little better rate of return than a savings account, although not much.

"The cons are twofold: a CD does lock your money away for a couple years, and it's not really very liquid, although you can often get loans by using it as collateral, if you need. Plus, the return isn't nearly as good as other investment options when it comes to combating inflation.

"The exciting thing about the market-linked CD is that you actually get a higher rate of return than a traditional CD because it's linked to the stock market performance."

"I'm not a risk taker, remember? The stock market makes me a little nervous."

"That's what is neat about this special type of market-*linked* CD," Brett explained. "You aren't actually risking your money in the market at all. It's still totally safe and guaranteed, but you get a little more potential growth if the market goes up because your growth is linked to the market. It's a cool way to structure a CD."

"Who guarantees it?"

"It's backed by a fully FDIC-insured bank— they've just been a bit more creative about how to structure them to allow for a higher rate of return. We'll talk a bit more about the idea of getting the ups of the market, with no downside risk. The growth can be much higher, even double, what a typical CD rate is."

"Okay, that sounds less frightening. I might even be getting a little bit excited."

"Yeah, just wait until I show you the next couple of options—they'll get you really excited. Keep in mind that not all banks can provide what I'm about to show you, and you'll want to speak with someone who knows about the nuances before you purchase one. If you're interested, speak with a trained representative first. You can find one by going to www.milliondollardiva.com. They can explain all your options. One I particularly like is called real estate hard money lending, but you're not ready for that yet. (This is *really cool*, and people with a nest egg already saved up can learn more about it at www.milliondollardiva.com.) Down the road, I'll refer you to someone to get you hooked up with that. For now, I want to tell you about two things that will really increase your investment potential. The first is called an indexed annuity, and it's a very popular and safe money tool for retirement."

"And you'll explain everything, right? Keep in mind, we're in totally unfamiliar territory for me right now."

"Of course. Just ask me anything you like as we go along. Twenty years ago, annuities got a bad rap from financial advisors selling them to seniors who didn't know what they were getting. Once the seniors passed away, their families would end up losing a large portion of their estates. The seniors, of course, never intended for that to happen, but they were scammed.

"Those days are gone. The annuity companies have made significant changes to their plans to make sure that can't happen anymore. Now there's usually a death benefit associated with the annuity, so if the owner dies, the family can get paid the entire amount.

"Annuities are awesome because they are safe, can be bought using qualified money from a 401(k) or IRA, and can give you great passive income. This is truly a powerful tool because your money is guaranteed by the insurance company, so it's never at risk in the market . . . and it can guarantee an income for life."

"And where does the indexing come in?" My husband is a genealogist, so I was pretty sure my definition of "indexing" and Brett's were going to be very different.

"You can get your annuity indexed so it goes up to a cap when the market goes up, but it never comes down. So every year your gains are locked in, and you can start going up again each year. On top of that, you can get a guaranteed income paid to you for the rest of your life. These programs are typically good for people approaching fifty-plus years old and have money dedicated for their retirement."

"I really like that idea," I said. My mind just kept going back to my grandma. I hate the idea of seniors being scammed and having nothing to live on. "401(k) plans don't have guaranteed income for life, do they?"

"No way. 401(k)s don't offer lifetime income options—they don't guarantee anything.

"I know I've given you a lot to think about, but let me throw a couple more things out there. You can even do many of these investments like annuities, buying gold and silver, and real estate, using money you have in qualified plans right now. So if you have money tied up in a 401(k) or IRA, you can roll it out into a self-directed IRA and be in control of it the whole time."

"Okay." I made a note. "What I'd like to do is meet with you again when my husband can be here, so we can discuss all this together. He's more of a math mind than I am, and he'd love to sit and crunch all the numbers with you."

"Absolutely. It's critical for long-term success that married couples to go through this process together, especially when it's combined family income that will be used to invest."

"Do you have anything a little simpler to start with?"

"I do, in fact. This last strategy is my favorite because it meets all six of our criteria, it's simple and easy, and it's loaded with all kinds of additional benefits."

"Is this the autopilot program you mentioned?"

"You guessed it. It's really called the 101 Plan™. It has become insanely popular, exploding with growth over the past several years because of all the benefits it offers. It's a modified cash value life insurance policy."

"What? You can make money with life insurance?"

"I knew you'd react like that . . . almost everyone does."

"I'm just a little confused, that's all. I thought life insurance was for when you die."

"It's so much more than that—trust me. This unique tool is loaded with benefits you'd probably never anticipate. If done right, it can offer safe, guaranteed growth every year . . . in fact, you can experience potential double-digit growth, 12% to even 17% on your money in the good years of the market, with zero risk of loss when the market crashes.

"It's a time-tested financial product that has been stable for over a hundred years.

"It's been untouched by major market crashes.

"It gives you tax-advantaged growth, meaning your money grows tax deferred, and you can access your money when you want it throughout your life, and in retirement, without a taxable event.

"It gives you access to your money so you can act as your own banker and pay for major purchases, vacations, college funding, or other needs. And instead of putting it on a credit card, you borrow from yourself and pay yourself back . . . with interest!

"Lastly, you can literally build a million-dollar tax-free supplemental retirement income using this strategy. It takes no financial expertise. No picking stocks, no dealing with brokers, and no worrying about the market ups and downs. If you invest adequately, you could take out millions in retirement.

"Plus, remember it *is* a life insurance policy, so as soon as your first premium payment is received, you now have a contract with an insurance company that will pay your family a death benefit that could be in the millions. Where else can you trade a $200 premium payment for a guarantee of one million dollars? You can't get that from the lottery. You'd just have two hundred lottery tickets."

"It sounds like it gives a lot of benefits all at once. How exactly does it work?"

"The cash value growth in your 101 Plan™ indexing policy is linked to a market index, like the S&P 500, for example. The S&P 500 is a grouping of large company stocks, and it's used as a general indicator of the market. But your cash is *not* actually invested *in* the market. That way, your money is always safe and guaranteed by the insurance company.

"Your money is protected from any market loss, but at the same time, you participate in the growth of the S&P 500 up to a limit or cap. Let's say the upside cap is 12%. This can vary from plan to plan. This means that even if the market goes up 14% or more, your cash value growth would be limited to just 12%.

"Having a cap is actually a good thing because this is what allows the insurance company to protect you against losses in those years when the market goes down.

"Let's look at a picture that illustrates this point. This is a hypothetical example of a typical stock market strategy vs. a 101 Plan™ indexing strategy.

"So, let's say you start out with $10,000, and in the first year, the S&P 500 grows by 10%. The first year, there is no difference, and you have $11,000 in either account. In year two, your money grows another 10%. Now you have $12,100 in either account.

"But let's say that in year three, the S&P 500 drops 20%. Can that happen? Sure it can. The last few years of the 2000s were worse than that! Now you would have about $9,600 if you had invested directly in the S&P 500. However, in the indexed strategy, your principal and interest are protected against market loss. So, now instead of $9,600, you hold at $12,100.

"In year four, the market drops another 17%. Now, instead of having $9,600, you have around

$7,900. In the indexed strategy, you're still on hold at $12,100.

"Now here's the million-dollar question: Do you want $7,900 or $12,100?

"That's quite a difference, and it's clear from this example that losing principal can be financially devastating. That's why Warren Buffet said, 'It's not so much about the return *on* your money as the return *of* your money.' When you lose principal, you've got to get big-time results to bring it back to even.

"Now let's look at what happens when the market rebounds. Let's say in year five the market grows by 15%. In the stock market strategy, the $7,900 would get the full 15% growth, which is about $1,100, so your cash value would climb back up to a little over $9,000. In the indexed strategy, your money would only grow by 12% (remember we have a cap) to $13,550. But even with the

capped growth, you have $13,550 versus $9,000! Again, quite a difference.

"In this example, the downsides of the stock market strategy were:

- After five years, you end up with less money than you started with.
- It will take a 30% return to get you back to your original $10,000 (and how likely is that to happen in *one* year?)

"Even if you did get the 30% you needed, it will only bring you back to $10,000. You just lost *five* years and you are just barely back to even.

"Can you see why the 101 Plan™ indexing strategy is so exciting? Now you can have your money growing when the market goes up, you could outpace inflation with potential double-digit gains, and you never have to worry about losing money when the market goes down.

"Now what would happen if the market goes down for ten years in a row?

"Many of the 101 Plan™ policies can be set up so there is a guaranteed amount of growth credited to your policy cash values, which guarantees that even if you don't achieve growth in the market, your cash value can continue to grow. But every plan is a little bit different. That's why it's so important to work with a trained representative who can show you your options."

I blinked. "You've been speaking a foreign language for the last few minutes, Brett. I'll need a trained representative just to act as an interpreter."

Brett laughed. "Sorry. Yes, when it's time to get you hooked up with investments, I will slow down and walk you through it a step at a time, making sure you understand exactly what's happening. For now, the most important thing for you to know is that you can use this strategy, and it's like autopilot. No stock charts or worrying about the market—just a simple process. And some of these financial products can even guarantee an income you will never outlive."

"What's the minimum amount of money I would need to start a 101 Plan™? And could it cover my whole family?"

"Great questions. You can get started for as little as $100 per month. As far as covering your whole family, the good news is that you can use the money for whatever you want. So you can pay for college, retirement, a new home, whatever. And remember, these policies are designed with the lowest death benefit possible to keep insurance costs low. So if you want insurance for your family, buying a term-life policy is usually much cheaper, and you can get a term-life policy that covers Mom, Dad, and a small death benefit for the kids to cover funeral expenses, all on one policy."

"You know we've had some health problems. Will that stop us from using this strategy?"

"Another very good question. The answer is yes and no. I don't know all the ins and outs of your health situation, but let's say for example that you personally can't qualify. You can do what is called 'borrow a life.' This means that you can take out the policy on a spouse, child, or grandchild, and you still own and control it. You get the benefits of the policy, but the insurance policy is on the child. This way, people with health problems can still use the 101 Plan™ for tax-deferred growth and tax-free income in retirement."

"That's great to know." I leaned back and glanced over the notes I'd been taking during our conversation. "We've talked about a lot of investment options. Do you think I should start with silver, or a 101 Plan™?"

"I recommend a 101 Plan™ because of two important factors—the time value of money, and compound interest. Silver can give you gains, but they aren't necessarily compounding each year on top of each other. Its value can go up dramatically at times, but it can come right back down. It's a great savings tool, but not a great retirement plan.

"When you get started in a 101 Plan™, your interest gains are locked in, and you are compounding your growth every year. Remember, Albert Einstein said, 'Compound interest is one of the most powerful forces in the Universe.' Let me show you an example.

"Let's say two people, Mark and Marcy, who are both twenty-two years old, look over their finances and discover an extra $2,000 in their budgets. Mark opens up a plan to start saving, but Marcy spends her money.

"Now let's say that Mark's plan earns 12% per year. He puts aside $2,000 per year for six years, and then decides he's done enough and doesn't invest any further.

"Meanwhile, Marcy has been spending her money, but after six years, she wises up and begins to invest. She puts $2,000 a month into a savings plan until she's 65 years old, and she's also getting 12%.

"Check out this chart—it shows how crucial it is to start your plan now:

Age	Mark	Marcy
22	$2,240	$0
23	4,509	0
24	7,050	0
25	9,896	0
26	13,083	0
27	16,653	0
28	18,652	2,240
29	20,890	4,509
30	23,397	7,050
35	41,233	25,130
40	72,667	56,993
45	128,064	113,147
50	225,692	212,598
55	397,746	386,516
60	700,965	693,879
65	1,235,339	1,235,557

"Look at how amazing this is. Mark only put in $12,000 *total*. That's $2,000 a year for six years. Marcy put in $74,000, which is six times as much money. Mark invested for six years, Marcy for 37, and they both have the same amount at retirement!"

"Wow," I said. "If Marcy finds out, she's going to be a little angry."

"As you can see, with compound interest, the earlier you start saving, the greater the interest on your original investment. The best time to start saving is now—no matter how large or small the amount. No delays, no procrastination."

"So, help me understand something." I leaned forward a little. "I've heard the debt gurus say things like, 'If you can save 20% by paying off debt, why would you put your money some place where it's only earning 12%?' What do you think about that?"

"Remember how we discussed in detail the fact that money isn't math . . . it's about emotion?"

"Yes."

"Well, what these microwave money gurus are telling you completely disregards two factors. The first is that time is crucial to growing your wealth. As we've seen, it's vital that you get started sooner rather than later. And once we put money away, it's less likely that we'll spend it because of the positive emotional charge we get from seeing our wealth grow. Just watching your debt go down is one thing, but watching wealth grow is much more exciting and energizing. Second, most people don't follow through on paying down their debts properly and then investing that money after they are paid off. They pay off high-interest debt, sure . . . but then what? They just keep spending the money. They don't have a plan to grow their wealth at that point. It's just back to the same negative emotional cycle of earn and spend, earn and spend.

"If this was all about math, then what they say makes sense. But it's not. That's why I recommend that *everyone*, regardless of their debt situation, make a commitment to start saving something immediately, even if it's just 1% of your income.

"One of the simplest, yet most profound, of the principles of true wealth is *pay yourself first*. You have to do this!

"You'll never make true financial progress until you start paying yourself by saving money. If that's fifty bucks a month, then buy an ounce of silver. If you can do more, then start a 101 Plan™. You've seen what happens when you go through the 'Give Yourself a Raise' session—you can find several hundred dollars per month you can start saving. We rarely have someone go through this process and not find at least $300 per month they are currently wasting."

I nodded. "Thanks for taking this time with me today, Brett. I think my mind has been opened to a lot of new possibilities."

"You're welcome. And remember, you can make an appointment with me any time if you'd like me to explain this further. My favorite part of my job is helping people empower themselves to get this process started. Are you ready?"

"Bring it on."

Chapter 10

FINANCES AND THE MARRIED WOMAN

My husband and I have experienced our ups and downs financially, as I mentioned earlier. Brett and Ethan asked us how money has affected our marriage, and what strain it's put on our relationship. That's a pretty tough question—because finances are so closely linked in to my sense of security, they also affect my relationships whenever money is involved.

"My feelings toward our money have changed quite a bit over the years that we've been married," I said after a few minutes of reflection. "Matt had some student loans and some credit card debt when we met, and as we were planning the wedding, he sat me down, showed me his debt payment chart, and explained that things would be tight for a while. I grew up without money, so the thought of being poor didn't scare me. There have been times, though, when his financial situation has really been hard for me. It has taken longer than we thought to pay off his debts—one student loan in particular may be with us forever, and we've had to apply for forbearance on it several times. I'll admit that I have felt a little accusatory at times because of it. We went through a really rough patch near the beginning of our marriage when we felt desperate, and I struggled to stay positive. Right now, though, I'm in a place where I realize that the past is the past, I've made mistakes, too, and I'm ready to focus on the future and create a better tomorrow for ourselves and for our family."

"What about you, Matt?" Ethan asked.

"Financial struggles come with a lot of pressure," Matt said. "It's harder to communicate because of that pressure, and it's easier to misunderstand each other because of the urgency to solve the problem *right now*. Lack of money increases despair and frustration, creates a sense of hopelessness, and creates apathy toward the situation.

"I've seen people give up the care of their family so they can earn more money, and I've never wanted that to be me. But the stress over debt makes me want to hide—often in addictive forms, with video games. Most often, the stress comes from dealing with the money itself rather than from dealing with Tristi about it. I've had momentary frustrations, and in the past I've felt like giving up—not on the marriage, but on ever getting out of debt. That's what I mean by hopelessness. When I look at our debt situation, it seems like we may never get out—especially with the way the economy is right now.

"But we've had a really good relationship, and in the back of my mind I've always known that in the morning things would be different, and I would have more resources to give it another try. We've been really blessed in that we are persistent, that we want to talk to each other, and that even when we feel like we want to give up, it's not a permanent thing. We can back off for a while and decide to come back to it after we have more of our marbles or when we are less tired."

"It sounds like the two of you have a pretty good handle on your relationship, even though there have been moments of stress," Brett commented.

"I'd say that's accurate," I replied. "And I do want to point out that some of our current debt is on my head—we have a couple of credit cards that I ran up when money was tight. So I don't blame Matt's student loans entirely for our situation. We both have ownership of this."

"It's good that you're both taking responsibility for how you contributed," Ethan said. "Far too often, when we work with married people, we hear them blame each other for their problems and refuse to admit how much they, themselves, have caused. They argue and accuse, and they make each other the enemy. The fact is, we shouldn't be fighting against our spouse—we should be fighting against interest, against bad investments, and we should be fighting to get out of debt."

"That can only happen as you learn to work together," Brett added. "Husbands and wives need to be playing on the same side. They need to see each other as teammates, not as the opposition. When we spend our time fighting, we're wasting energy. We should be using our energy to solve our problems, not blaming each other for causing the problem in the first place."

"I love my husband a lot," I said, "and when I realized that I was unfairly blaming him for our debt load, and I realized how hard he works every day to support us, I felt really bad about the times when I'd been too hard on him about it."

"We all make mistakes." Matt reached out and took my hand. "I thought getting a degree would help me support my family, so I ran up those student loans. Tristi ran up some credit cards because we needed groceries and diapers. We were both trying to do the right thing, and sure, we didn't go about it the right way, but our hearts were in the right place. It's hard to hold grudges when you know someone is doing the best they can."

"That's the key right here," Brett said. "The biggest hurdle for couples is getting on the same page financially. Once that happens, you stop feeling like you are competing against each other, and you can turn your focus to the true enemy.

"We're going to give you the critical information and the tools you need to create the future you want, together. Keep your relationship central to everything you do," Brett said.

"We mentioned working as a team," Ethan continued. "That's the first step. Every married couple should sit down and talk things over, and make a pact that no matter what happens, you will approach it together. No more keeping secrets from each other, no more feeling ashamed of your past actions. The key is knowing what your *true* goal is together. One of you can't be thinking the priority is to get out of debt and pay off the house, and the other thinking how can we afford to get that new car. This is a new beginning, a fresh start. Think of this as a blank slate—your actions from here on out will determine your future."

"If you're not on the same page, you just can't be successful," Brett added. "You might have a great day tracking your expenses and keeping within your spending plan, but your spouse might do some impulse shopping and throw everything off. In the money game, you simply can't afford to be competing with each other.

"There are a ton of stories of teams, armies, and organizations who were supposed to be working together against the competition, but because of quarrels in their organization, they actually defeated themselves from within. We even see it throughout history—for instance, right after World War I, China's two major parties, one led by Mao Zedong and the other by Chiang Kai-shek, tried to form an alliance to rule the country, but they weren't on the same page. They had different goals for China, and soon they were battling against each other. Chiang had superior fighting power, but his men had started quarreling amongst themselves, and they didn't form a united front against Mao. Guess who won?"

"I'm somewhat of a historian, so I knew it was Mao," I replied. "But I didn't know about all the quarreling going on behind the scenes. That really does weaken your defenses, whether you're a family or a nation."

"It's critical that you don't let this happen within your marriage or you'll never win out," Brett said. "You absolutely must be on the same page. If you decide together what you're going to spend and how much you're going to save, you'll reach your goals more quickly, and you'll find that working together makes your marriage stronger, too."

Ethan leaned forward. "When you have these discussions about spending, compromise and stay calm. Decide what you most need, decide what you most want, and be gentle with each other. If your spouse makes a suggestion that you really don't like, state that calmly and then suggest what you would like to see happen. As you talk it out and discuss pros and cons, you'll find the right compromises for your budget and for your relationship. Let go of the shame and guilt and focus on the future, not the past.

"As much as we'd like to ignore the truth sometimes, success comes from making accurate decisions. And accurate decisions come from addressing the world as it is, not as we'd like it to be. Healthy finances are the core of a healthy relationship. Not that you have to be wealthy, but you can't be in debt and constantly harassed by creditors and short on food money, and have a healthy family."

"We've recently taped a piece of paper to our bedroom wall where we write down everything we've spent," Matt said. "We track it in the checkbook ledger, too, but when it's up on the wall where we both can see it, we can know at a glance exactly where we are."

"It helps with the accountability you were talking about," I added. "And I appreciate what you said about letting go of the shame and the guilt—I've struggled with that a lot. I'm not an extravagant person—I rarely buy things we don't need—but when I do, I have a hard time not feeling as though I've done something really wrong."

"There's nothing wrong with buying wants when you've worked out a spending plan with your spouse," Brett said. "In fact, everyone should have an amount they can spend without feeling guilty.

"Something that helped me and my wife years ago was going to an all-cash budget for her expenses, like the groceries, kids' stuff, gas for the car, etc," Brett said. "It was a perfect solution because she could always see how much she had. When she was out, she was out, and there were no overdraft fees to pay at the end of the month.

"Also, look into a line of credit on your checking account. Just $500 to $1000 can help avoid the bounced check fees with overdraft protection, and it would save you not only money, but hassle."

"One thing that has helped me and my wife, Erika, is separating the tracking duties," Ethan said. "For example, she takes ownership of deciding how much to spend each month for food, clothes, and stuff for the kids. She collects all the receipts, calculates them, and makes sure we don't spend more than our limit. I have the responsibility of other categories. When we meet each month to go over the finances, we start on an even playing field since we both have ownership in the process. It has helped our communication when it comes to money, and strengthened our relationship."

"So, what do you tell couples who fight about money a lot?" I asked. "I have friends who just can't see eye-to-eye about it, and sometimes they really say mean things to each other."

Brett shifted a little in his chair. "I see this happen a lot, and more often than not, it's caused by the fact that the husband and wife are not really trying to accomplish the same things. We've already talked at length about this, but it bears repeating. People fight about money because one person doesn't think they can afford something the other spouse bought. It can be either husband or wife, but what often happens is that one of the spouses is much more concerned, careful, and mindful of money than the other. It's really frustrating, then, when the woman of the house is trying to save everywhere and anywhere she can, and the husband comes home with a new golf club he didn't really need, and it cost $150."

"We've had a few struggles in that area ourselves—not with golf clubs, but other things," I said. "And I know that financial problems often lead to divorce."

"The National BAR Association shows that finances are a leading cause cited in divorces," Ethan said. "But it's not the money itself that leads to divorce—it's selfishness. If the husband puts his needs ahead of his wife's, or vice versa, and they start hiding transactions from each other or feeling entitled to their extra purchases, it does put a strain on the relationship. The problem isn't so much the money as it is the attitude toward money. It's clearly essential to get this right."

"I want to add something important about the completely misleading stats thrown around about divorce rates, and the fact that marriage often makes people more financially successful," Brett said. "Everyone quote statistics about how 50% of all marriages end in divorce, but it's flawed math. It's not true that half of all people who get married get divorced."

I thought about that for a second. "What do you mean exactly?"

"Let's take a hundred people, for example, and let's say they all get married at the same time.

According to this misleading stat, you'd think that 50% of them would end up getting divorced, right?

"Right."

"Well, it's not accurate. Here's why. Studies have shown that people who have been divorced once have a tendency to get divorced multiple times. My mother-in-law has a friend who was on *The Dr. Phil Show* because she's been married and divorced eleven times. Her most recent marriage was supposed to be the last one, and Dr. Phil paid for marriage counseling *before* they tied the knot, just to give them the best chance. Any guesses on what happened?"

"I'll take a wild shot in the dark and say she got divorced again," I replied.

"You got it. They lasted about eleven days before they separated.

'Now let me share with you another interesting statistic. Dr. Thomas Stanley, the author of *The Millionaire Next Door*, shows in his study of tens of thousands of millionaires that the overwhelming majority are married, and have not ever been divorced. They figured out a way to work together to successfully build a marriage and financial foundation together.

"The mainstream media disparages marriage and wants people to believe that marriage is a waste of time. They promote the idea that marriage 'clearly doesn't work' because 50% fail. But of *our* one hundred test cases, twenty may end up getting divorced—some once, some twice, and several even three or more times. This accounts for fifty total divorces, but eighty of the hundred may still be happily married!"

"That makes sense," Matt said. "Those statistics always have seemed off to me."

"So back to the issue of how to make this work for couples who are fighting over money," Brett said. "I'm not a real big fan of marriage counseling—I think you'll find that once you do a couple of simple things that we talk about, your relationship will improve dramatically.

"The foundation of making this successful is to get on the same side of the ball, get on the same team, get on the same page—however you want to say it. I'm a guy, so I think in terms of sports. But if you're the football field, and the wife is on offense and husband is on defense, you're smashing into each other day in and day out, and that's not a fun relationship.

"You have to talk about what is important to each of you. If the other spouse doesn't want to address the issue, you have to force it. This is too important to leave to chance, and you can't be financially successful alone.

"Ask your husband to talk about what you are trying to accomplish financially for at least five to ten minutes. Tell him it's critically important to you, and if you approach it in the right way, in a kind way, he will give you the time—just don't ask him during the ball game.

"Together, answer the question: what are we trying to accomplish? Are we trying to save up to go on a trip somewhere, to pay off the car, to put money away each month so we can retire someday and buy a vacation home? What are we trying to do?

"Once you know that, it becomes much, much easier. The solution to fighting over money is tracking your spending.

"It's not about how much you make. It's about how much you keep. I know many doctors who make close to a million dollars per year, and they spend it all. They're in a worse financial situation than folks making $40,000 per year.

"Review your spending every week and make sure you pace yourself so you have money for the end of the month. We use a Smartphone app called Expense Tracker to do it all very quickly, and that works well for us.

"It's amazing the refreshing and empowering feeling you'll have once you're tracking your spending and you know how much money you have left to spend.

"Irreverent as it may seem, in my 'first life' as a struggling, worried salesperson, we didn't have a lot of money. And we didn't have any of these tips figured out, either. I still remember sitting in bed late at night with the calculator, crunching numbers and trying to balance the family budget—we didn't have a federal bailout for my finances. Needless to say, arguing about money, being worried about debts, and feeling guilty about spending too much does not create the ideal marriage.

"But once your finances are under control, once you are on the same side working toward the same goal, you become energized about your plan. Life is fun and enjoyable, and you aren't feeling guilty or fighting over the money. And it makes the love life a lot more . . . shall we say . . . lively.

"That's the best advice I can give to anyone fighting over money. Make sure you are working toward the same goals, then track your spending and be sure to address it every week or two so you don't get too far off track. And whatever you do, keep your relationship first. All the financial success in the world doesn't matter if you've lost the one you love most."

Chapter 11

AMPLIFY YOUR INCOME

"Mom, you got a package." My seven-year-old handed me a large envelope, and I read the return address label—*Safe Money Millionaire*. This was the Income Amplifier Brett had promised to send me, and I was excited to open it. The Safe Money Millionaire guys had already taught me some amazing things—I knew this product would blow my mind even more.

Brett told me it was the process they use to help people create a little extra income outside of their regular job. They used it to start their own companies, which have now done millions in sales. He said he knew it would help us increase our income, because even just an extra $500 per month would go a long way for us.

In fact, looking at the Drive Down plan and the opportunity to pay off our debt to build wealth was really inspiring. It made my husband and me both want to increase our income so we could make it all happen faster. Needless to say, I was interested to see what it was all about.

When my husband got home that night, he and I sat down and opened the envelope. It contained two cases of CDs and a workbook, which was filled with charts and worksheets. We decided to look over the materials together, then approach the worksheets from our own unique perspectives. I'm an author and an editor, and I want to maximize my business and my earning potential while creating more time for my family. Matt's a genealogist who also takes on private clients, and he's writing a book to teach people how to do their own family history. He wants to make enough money to get out of debt while doing something he loves—helping people trace their family trees.

The CDs were full of great information and touched on things we never would have envisioned for ourselves. We listened to Brett and Ethan set the framework by discussing some of the key principles of debt management and then head into the core lesson—how to amplify your income so you can get out of debt faster and start saving for your future.

I was really impressed by the true stories we heard of average people, single moms, grandmas, even fathers moonlighting and everything in between, who are earning more money. All it takes is some motivation and a little work to make extra income that they control. They aren't asking a boss for a raise—if they want more money, they go earn it.

At the front of the workbook is a list of all kinds of skill sets that can be turned into additional income. Of course the list isn't complete—it would be an entire volume all by itself if it was—but it showed things both Matt and I have done in the past and enjoyed doing, and was a springboard for launching other ideas in our minds.

Matt took note of all the computer-related jobs, and of course saw the mention of "genealogy specialist," while I gravitated toward the writing jobs—no surprise there. We both also noticed things we were good at, but hadn't considered doing for income. As we thought about those things, though, we realized that maybe we were holding ourselves back a little and weren't fully exploring all the possibilities we'd been given.

"I could do several of the things on that list," Matt said, "and I'd enjoy most of them. I thought of a few others that weren't included, too. I really feel that genealogy is my path, so that's the one I'll explore further. Okay, what do we do next?"

"We need to think about using our spare time to bring in some extra money, and we need to be thinking of ways to market our skills more effectively," I replied. "We want to encourage people to come to us when they have a need in one of these areas, and not someone else."

"They said we should focus on solving people's problems, because people are eager to get rid of the problems in their lives," Matt said. "How do we remind them that they have a problem, and then encourage them to come to us to fix it?"

"Let's brainstorm your business for a minute," I suggested. "What are the problems people face when it comes to doing their genealogy?"

As we talked, we came up with this list:

- Genealogy is hard.
- I don't know how to use the computer to do my genealogy.
- I don't know how to read the language my great-great-grandparents spoke.
- I can't figure out the name changes and misspellings that were made when the records were kept.
- I don't know how to find and use online databases.
- I can't read my ancestor's handwriting.
- I don't have time.

"I think the last one is probably the biggest stumbling block," I said. "Family history work isn't a quick endeavor, and very few people have the time to spend on it."

"And I'd say they also perceive it as being hard," Matt replied. "So we have seven solid reasons why people don't want to do their genealogy, and we've narrowed it down to the two most common ones."

"Great. Now let's think about all the ways in which you are the right person to help solve their problem."

We pulled out another piece of paper and jotted down a list of reasons why Matt was the ideal choice. He is:

- Knowledgeable
- Educated
- Logical
- Experienced

"That's a great start. We can add more later—I'm sure more ideas will come." I looked at the list, then back at my husband. "Okay, now we need to decide why your potential clients should like you."

"That's right—the likeability factor."

Brett and Ethan had spoken about how successful businesses are often driven by a personality that is likeable—Dave Thomas with Wendy's, Oprah, Papa John's Pizza, or Colonel Sanders with Kentucky Fried Chicken. Customers don't want to shell over their hard-earned money to someone they don't like. I like my husband plenty, but now we needed to define why other people would like him too—for very different reasons.

Matt's likeable traits are:

- Compassion
- Persistence
- Honesty
- Understanding
- Thoroughness
- Friendliness
- Flexibility

"I think I'd enjoy working with someone who had all these traits," I said. "I might marry them, too, but that could just be me."

Matt smiled, and then we turned our attention back to the assignment. "So, we've chosen the skill set you're going to amplify, which is genealogy, and we've identified why your potential clients would struggle to do it for themselves," I said. "We know why you're a great choice for the job, and we know why people will like you. The next step is linking all that together."

We'd been taught while listening to the Income Amplifier that the right kind of advertising was going to be key to getting new clients, and we should take the information we'd just written down and use it for our hook, or our slogan, to bring people in. I pulled out the Fill-in-the-Blank Headline Formulas in the Income Amplifier workbook.

"Remember, focus on the problem first," I said. "Remind people they have a problem, and you can solve it."

We tossed around ideas for a few minutes, some of them decent and some just way too corny.

"I've got it," Matt said. "'Were your ancestors the strong, silent type? They were strong—they pioneered new lands. They were silent—they left no records behind.'"

I laughed. "That would be great in the book you're writing, honey, but maybe a little long for an advertising hook. How about, 'Has your family tree got you stumped?'"

"That could work. Let's write it down, and add to our list as more ideas come."

I jotted it down. "And how can you solve their problems? How can you be their Superman?"

"I wouldn't look good in tights, but I could do a cape."

I shook my head. "No man looks good in tights, honey. Let's stick with the cape."

Matt agreed. "Okay—why should they come to me? I could tell them, 'I can save you time, I can save you energy, I can save you technical hassles, I can solve your language problems, and I can help you outline your family's successes.'"

"That's great—I think you just addressed each of the excuses they would have for not doing their own family history work. Let's think about the two main reasons we identified—genealogy is hard, and it's time consuming."

"Okay—I can save them time, and I can make it easy."

I nodded. "I think that would answer their need. So, we've identified their pain, we've spoken to their pain, and we've presented the trustworthy solution—you. Now we need to decide the best way to get clients."

"The Income Amplifier gave me a lot of great ideas, but there were three that stood out to me," Matt said. "I loved the idea of putting up a commercial on YouTube. That would give me the chance to show people who I am as a person, which would build up that likeability factor. I'd make it really professional, but also down to earth."

"I like that, too," I said, wondering why I hadn't thought of that before. Okay, I knew why—Brett and Ethan are masters at having great ideas, and they'd been surprising me for months with great idea after great idea.

"The second was to use word of mouth. People tell people when they've had really emotional experiences, good and bad. I can ask my clients if they would refer me to their friends and family."

"I know how powerful word of mouth can be," I replied. "That's definitely the way the world works. What was the third strategy?"

"Registering on a site such as Guru.com, elance.com or odesk, or peopleperhour. There are a lot of opportunities to get clients with no advertising costs at all. I could see myself creating a nice profile with my resumé, and drawing in clients just through the virtue of those sites."

"And then we'll use the additional money you bring in to drive down our debts, as we charted out on the Drive Down program."

"Exactly. So, how can we use the Income Amplifier to monetize your business?"

I thought about that for a minute. My business was already doing well, but I knew I could do more to make it profitable. "I think I need to change my course of direction," I said. "I'm spending a lot of time doing things that don't bring in as much income, and they're taking my time away from the larger, more lucrative jobs."

"I've wondered about that," Matt said. "So you're going to cut back your business so you can grow it? Sounds like it wouldn't work, but that's how you prune a tree—you get rid of the little parts that aren't working so the whole tree can grow stronger."

"Yes, that's what I mean," I said. "And I feel really good about this decision. I'm going to finish up the small tasks I have now, and then refer my clients to other qualified professionals when they need additional small tasks. I want to focus on the bigger picture, and this will allow me to retrain that focus."

"What are those smaller tasks?" Matt asked.

"Virtual book tours, for one. They're a lot of fun to coordinate, but they're so time-consuming, I sometimes feel I'm paying the author for the privilege instead of making the income I need." I paused as lightning shot through my brain. "Wait—

hold on. I just had a great idea. Instead of just retiring from tours, I'll write a book about how to organize them. That will become a product I can sell that will produce passive income, like the guys have been talking about. I write the book once, and it brings me income multiple times."

"That's a great idea," Matt said.

My brain was still buzzing. "And that's not all. I could write books about blogging and homeschooling. I could turn my online writing instruction course into a workbook. If I invest a little time now to get those books written and produced, I could save myself a lot of time later that I could then invest in the more important projects—editing and ghostwriting for my clients, and writing my own books." I laughed. "I might even spend some time with you and the kids once in a while."

"That would be great. You have been really busy lately. And didn't your doctor say you needed to spend less time at the computer?"

"Yeah, he's worried that I won't heal up as quickly from the car accident if I don't find ways to rest more."

"Then this sounds like a perfect plan."

It really did sound perfect, and I was starting to get excited. Ideas for marketing were pouring into my head, as well as possible covers, titles, and topics. I took a second to e-mail a friend who could help me format my books for Kindle, and another friend who could help us film the YouTube video for Matt.

As the evening progressed, I noticed that Matt seemed more upbeat. "So what do you think of all this?" I asked him.

"I feel hopeful," he replied. "I'm really looking forward to taking the skills I have and monetizing them in such a way that we can increase our income and get out of debt—when we got married, I didn't think we'd ever get out of debt, but now we know how, and we have a plan. I feel liberated."

"And I feel more in control, which I love," I added. "We now have a target, and we have ammunition. This is kind of a power trip, really, power and a proven plan to change our lives."

Want to see if Matt and Tristi have been successful with their ideas?

Watch the Pinkstons put their plans into action

by visiting:

www.milliondollardiva.com

Chapter 12

MAKING IT WORK FOR YOU

"Guys, I'm so excited about everything I've learned from you," I told Brett and Ethan. "Matt and I have been making phone calls on our car insurance, we've been researching credit cards, and we're going in to talk to the bank next week. We've got plans to amplify our income—and the best part is that they're concrete plans. We have appointments to ask questions—we aren't just toying with asking questions. We're really going to do it."

"That's great," Brett said. "You've just summed up everything that's most important to us—you have hope, you have plans, and you're excited. When we can help someone get to that point, that's really our payoff right there."

"I have a question, though. Matt and I are working through this together, amplifying our dual incomes and leaning on each other for support and additional ideas. But what about my mom, who's nearing retirement age, and is a widow? Or what about my friend, who is a successful career woman, but hasn't ever been married? We come from three different circles of life, and I can see how this is going to work for me, but what about them? Will this system be as effective in their lives as it's going to be for me?"

"You're right that every woman's situation is unique," Ethan said. "The things we've discussed with you will provide insight for every woman who wants to become a Million Dollar Diva, but we would be foolish to think that a young woman eighteen to twenty-nine years in age has the same problems and situation as a woman of forty to sixty or a woman of sixty to eighty. The earlier you get started, the better—however, it's never too late to start. Let's take a look at some of the different stages of life that confront women today and some ways to help develop a solid plan for tomorrow.

"First, let's start with women who are eighteen to twenty-nine. This is still a wide age gap, and no two situations will be identical. Yet all women in this age group have a huge asset on their side—time. During this period, many will complete school and even get an upper graduate degree. In fact, more women are graduating from college now than ever before. More women are entering the work force and seeing huge success from starting their own business to increasing their wages working with a company."

"This brings to my mind the problem of student loans," Brett said. "Student debt is becoming a massive problem in our country. Kids are graduating from college with huge debt loads and not being able to pay them off, so their futures are crippled from the start. It's even worse in a bad economy when wages are down and unemployment is high, even for college graduates."

"I told you about Matt's experience," I replied. "He spent years in college and racked up a ton of debt getting his degree, only to find that it wasn't worth anything in the job market."

"That definitely does happen, and now you're left paying off those loans," Brett said. "One thing we tell everyone—if you have kids or grandkids preparing for college, do them a huge favor by helping them understand in black and white exactly how much their monthly debt load will be´once they graduate, if they go crazy and rack up student debt. In most cases, it really is not essential to get into debt to complete college. Get your education, but get it at the lowest cost possible. Once you graduate, it should be like a track star at the Olympics hearing that starting gun and taking off sprinting into the race. Starting your career and life and family with student debt is like a sprinter trying to run with shackles on her ankles.

"And as you know, it carries over into your marriages. Your kids go without because you have student loan debt, and it causes problems in the relationship. "

"Other young women will decide to start a family, which places them in a more complex role as a working professional and mother," Ethan continued. "My wife got her upper graduate degree and has continued working part-time as we've grown a family and I've pursued my career. Having the extra income is nice, but it also puts more time constraints on the family. It has required us to be more understanding of roles and scheduling of time. Many families are faced with the same dilemma.

"Even though this is a super busy stage of life, it's a great time to get on the Million Dollar Diva path. If you start now and stick to the blueprint, your chances of actually becoming a millionaire are greatly increased. Can you still arrive if you start later? Of course, but it may require you to sacrifice and put away a lot more in savings.

"Because more women are working today and starting businesses, this is a great time to get the best financial education you can. It can be hard to see ten or twenty years into the future, but it's vital that you take a step back and make a plan, following the simple guidelines we've outlined in this book. It doesn't matter if you're recently married, single, divorced, or separated. Having a plan for the future will allow you combat the financial challenges of life. And the same principles always apply. Start today to pay yourself first. And put it into a wise savings strategy . . . not risky investments."

"I heard someone say that you're able to risk more when you're younger because you have more time to make it back," I said. "I'm guessing you have some thoughts on that, based on everything we've been discussing."

"We have to consider the source," Brett said. "Who's been saying that? The investing guys, because they want you to invest in the market. Of course you're welcome to do with your money as you please, but I just had a conversation earlier with a young couple in their thirties. The husband has been at the same job, contributing to a 401(k) for twelve years. Any guesses on how much his money has grown in twelve entire years?"

"If I know you, this is a trick question," I said.

"Yeah, it is," Brett replied. "His money hasn't grown at all—in fact, he's lost money in his 401(k). What good did it do him to start the fund twelve years ago when it's shrinking in value? He's lost all that time because it's a losing strategy."

"Now let's talk about women in the middle stage of life, ages thirty to forty," Ethan said. "Many of the rules for younger women apply here, too. You still have a decent amount of time on your side to let your money grow safely.

"If you started building on a safe foundation in your early years, now it's about staying the course. Finding the Million Dollar Diva path might be easy, but sticking to it may be the hard part. If you have not yet started, use the tools in this book and create a solid plan for your future."

"This is the time of life when expenses crank up," Brett Said. "Bigger houses, larger cars, expensive kids, trips, peer pressure to compete with friends and neighbors to increase your standard of living, and letting expenses eat up any increase in income. This is where people get into huge credit card debt and go way off course. This is also where having a plan printed off and in plain sight so you can see it every day will help you stay on track and have the motivation to get that house paid off, and stay out of debt.

"There's something addictive about seeing your wealth grow every month. It's a lot of fun. It strengthens marriages and families, too—these financial victories set you up for a lifetime of happy memories."

"Now let's look at women in the age range of forty to sixty," Ethan said. "Their unique situation sets them apart from both younger and older women. As they enter the later phases in their life, they will reach a financial crossroads. Time has now become more of a premium. Once again, it's never too late to start and set up your family and future generations to win financially. However, you may have to sacrifice some wants to reach your goals.

"Women who range in age from forty through sixty lead multi-faceted, multi-stage lives. Their children grow up and allow them to have more time and money to undertake more interests. Goals may change at this stage in life. For example, in addition to securing a solid retirement, a woman in this stage may want to go back to school, start a business, travel more, or revisit a passion."

"There's also the pressure to help children who are starting families," Brett added. "This can be a touchy subject with people, but I think it's important to talk about it for a second. We discussed earlier the dangers of entitlement. We all want to be generous to our children and our grandchildren, but we need to be sure that we're not entitling them or giving them something for nothing. Everyone needs to learn the value of work. It's wonderful to be able to help your adult children out of a tight spot, but if you bail them out every single time they have a problem, they never will learn important life lessons for themselves."

"Very true," Ethan said. "I think a lot of retired parents deal with those very issues, and retired women face even more issues today than in the past. Extended female life expectancy causes the number of years that savings and income must stretch to go up, there are increased healthcare costs and long-term care expenses, and the dangers of carrying debt into retirement. Social Security could potentially go insolvent, and there are problems in relying on a spouse's pension and health benefits."

"In addition, there's the scenario of wives living longer than husbands," Brett added. "This is why life insurance is *crucial* to any sound financial plan. Like it or not, we're *all* going to die. The question is, are we going to let our loved ones and families become financially destitute because of our irresponsible behavior?

"I'll never forget the call I got from a client's wife. This really did happen—I was his risk management consultant for his contracting business, and his wife called and asked if by chance he had life insurance. I said no—I had recommended it to him multiple times, but he never paid the premiums to get it going.

"She told me he had just died of brain cancer and left her with a business she didn't know how to run, with several pieces of equipment with loans on them, a mortgage, car payments, two kids, and now funeral expenses. He was twenty-eight years old.

"His wife and family were devastated. But even worse, they had the additional crisis of bankruptcy, losing their house, cars, and everything they owned. No spouse should ever have to deal with that."

"That's awful." I imagined for a minute what it would be like to lose Matt suddenly. He's older than I am by fifteen years, and given the fact that women live longer than men, I could potentially be alone for a long time at the end of my life. I've already accepted this, but how would I feel if something happened to him long before then? I'm grateful for the life insurance policy we picked up several years ago, which will at least help me and the kids to stay on our feet.

"According to the 2005 Women & Investing Survey, 95% of women say that saving for retirement is the primary investment goal, yet 47% are not contributing a retirement plan," Ethan said. "That's why it's critical to act today. You can start with the tools and strategies in this book, visit our website www.milliondollardiva.com, and talk to a qualified representative to get you on the right path.

"Lastly, if you're a women sixty-plus years in age, this is a very unique time of life. You mentioned that your mother falls into this category?"

"That's right," I replied.

"Many women in this age group have money in a savings account or some retirement plan. At this stage in life, it's all about the preservation of income. If you're set up with a solid plan to never outlive your money, congratulations. If not, then you should continue to educate yourself on how to stretch income and savings during this time."

"I know my mom's going to want more information," I said. "I've been telling her about the process as I've learned about it, and I think she could really benefit from some additional advice."

"Send her on over," Brett said. "We'd love to help her out. Now, we spoke briefly about annuities and the guaranteed income you can receive from them. These are particularly valuable in a situation where there is some money in a retirement account. You can roll that money into some incredibly powerful financial tools, without fines or penalties, and get yourself an income for as long as you live. It's kind of like your own personal pension plan. Having a trusted representative will allow you to be more knowledgeable and confident about having enough money for the future.

"It truly is amazing what you can do in just five or ten years following a solid plan. Even if it means working a couple of extra years past the time you wanted to retire, those years can be the tipping point to setting yourself up for life. Women in this situation shouldn't let their circumstances discourage them. The proper education and help can truly change their lives.

"These ladies may want to consider finding a way to continue generating income and keeping certain skills sharp. Not many people want to continue working into their later years, but if it will help you reach your goals in the short-term, it may be a smart decision."

"And using the Income Amplifier to identify those skills and then market them," I added. "I'm really surprised by how much I learned listening to that program."

"Exactly," Ethan said. "The main thing to always consider is that it is *never* too late to start. You may not be able to accomplish as much in five years as you could in thirty. However, you can change your situation for the better, even reach many of your goals, and provide a solid financial future for your posterity."

* * *

Some final thoughts . . . I came into this situation feeling as though things were never going to change for me. When I met Brett and Ethan for the first time in my capacity as an editor for their project, I thought, "These guys are pretty nice." But I didn't have any expectation that I would so greatly benefit from the skills and principles they teach people all the time. I thought I'd just be editing their materials, collecting my check, and calling it a day.

But as we started talking, and they learned about my financial situation, they opened up their world to me, and I honestly can't believe how much my outlook has changed. It really has. I'm not saying that just because it sounds good in this book—although, it *does* sound good in this book. I'm saying it because I genuinely mean it. I've gone from feeling totally hopeless to feeling empowered. Will it take some guts to pull this off? Yes. Will I have to make some phone calls, move some credit cards around, get some loans, and be a little uncomfortable for a few minutes? Yes. Will I need to be more diligent, more focused, more committed than ever before? Yes. But every single bit of it is doable. Each step has been laid out for me. Each marker along my path has been clearly set up, and all I have to do is follow that path. It's up to me—but it always *has* been up to me.

The atmosphere in my home over the course of the last few days has changed remarkably. As Matt and I have discussed our Drive Down plan and spoken about amplifying our income, we have become excited. We're working together on a common goal instead of complaining about a common problem. When the parents are hopeful, the kids are hopeful. There's energy around here that's been missing for a long time.

I didn't agree to write this book so I could spout out a bunch of feel-good platitudes and then go on my merry—or not-so-merry—way. I agreed to write this book because I wanted this knowledge. I wanted to learn it, live it, and have a genuine experience with it. I'm committed to following this plan, and I want to share my commitment with you.

If you'll join me on www.milliondollardiva.com, you'll see regular updates from me. I will show you what I've done that week or that month to get out of debt. When I pay off a card, you'll know about it. If I have a setback, you'll know about it. I intend to get real about this, and I believe in accountability—when I began my weight loss journey last year, I invited my blog readers to follow my progress. I want to do the same thing with my financial journey. This isn't hype. This isn't one of my fiction novels, cleverly designed to sell financial products—this is real, and I would love to have your support. It's working for me, and it could work for you, too—come with me. Journeys are always more fun when you make them with friends.

ABOUT THE AUTHORS

Brett Kitchen is a co-author of the national Inc. Magazine bestseller *Safe Money Millionaire*. His family tree of entrepreneurship dates back to his great-great-great-grandfather, a watchmaker on Jersey Island off the coast of England. He has created two million-dollar businesses and has coached thousands of financial and insurance representatives on how to help people grow rich safely. Financial problems destroying families have caused Brett to help change the way Americans save and invest their money.

Visit Brett at:
www.SafeMoneyMillionaire.com

Tristi Pinkston is the author of eight novels, two cookbooks, one religious inspirational book, and over two thousand articles. She works full-time from home as a freelance editor, and is a featured presenter at writing conferences all over the Intermountain West. Tristi enjoys mentoring fledgling writers and helping them rise to their full potential as published authors.

You can learn more about her at:
www.tristipinkston.com

Ethan Kap is a leading expert in changing the way American families save and invest their money. He is the creator of a nationally recognized website www.SafeMoneyMillionaire.com, the co-author of the best-selling book, *Safe Money Millionaire*, and co-founder of the Safe Millionaire Academy. He is adamant about teaching others to take ownership of their financial destiny instead of being hooked on handouts and entitlements. Ethan is also a serial entrepreneur and has coached thousands of business owners to success.

Visit

www.milliondollardiva.com

today to receive:

- A free Safe Money Millionaire Blueprint
- A free download of the spending plan
- A link to the Expense Tracker App
- A free test drive of the Drive Down Debt Analysis software and Wealth Builder Blueprint

All the tools you need
to start your journey to financial freedom
are at your fingertips.